D1311581

# EARLY ADOLESCENCE

## Understanding the 10 to 15 Year Old

# EARLY ADOLESCENCE

## Understanding the 10 to 15 Year Old

### Gail A. Caissy

Foreword by
Conrad F. Toepfer, Jr.

**INSIGHT BOOKS**

PLENUM PRESS • NEW YORK AND LONDON

Library of Congress Cataloging-in-Publication Data

Caissy, Gail A.
    Early adolescence : understanding the 10 to 15 year old / Gail A.
  Caissy ; foreword by Conrad F. Toepfer, Jr.
        p.    cm.
    Includes bibliographical references and index.
    ISBN 0-306-44762-2
    1. Adolescent psychology.  2. Adolescence.  3. Educational
  psychology.    I. Title.
    BF724.C25   1994
    155.5--dc20                                                94-28521
                                                                   CIP

ISBN 0-306-44762-2

© 1994 Plenum Press, New York
A Division of Plenum Publishing Corporation
233 Spring Street, New York, N.Y. 10013-1578

*An Insight Book*

Printed in the United States of America

In memory of my mother

Irene Caissy

# Foreword

During the past four decades, I have shared in raising my own children and have also taught young adolescents, researched them, and worked with those who teach them. While I thoroughly enjoy young adolescents, many people do not and find them exasperating. Our understanding of young children is of less help as they approach and enter adolescence. Adults seem to better tolerate young adolescents as we better understand them, but fewer sources are available to help us understand them than there are about either elementary or high school-aged youth. The resultant combination of fact and folklore causes many parents and teachers to develop considerable misgivings about early adolescents.

*Early Adolescence: Understanding the 10 to 15 Year Old* will help parents, teachers, and other adults to better understand young adolescents. Gail Caissy's insightful book should substantially raise their knowledge about early adolescents and their educational needs. The author's invitational style makes this important information all the more beneficial. The introduction sets a "user-friendly" but definitive approach to the excellent, current information which Caissy develops throughout the book.

Part I offers significant insight about young adolescents for parents and beginning middle-grade teachers. Chapters 1–8 clearly define and discuss young adolescent physical, emotional, social, and intellectual development. Chapters 1, 3, 5, and 7 focus on the nature of each of those areas. The intervening chapters (2, 4, 6, and 8) effectively discuss the characteristics from each previous chapter in realistic, applied circumstances.

Parents should find Chapters 4 and 6 of particular value. The former carefully separates fact from folklore to build a better understanding of the emotional fluctuations common at that age. The latter describes the vacillating efforts of youth as they try to move toward independence. Chapter 9 effectively describes how more stable child–parent relationships established during children's elementary school years are often disrupted by the onset of early adolescence. Caissy dispels potential concerns that can develop about young adolescent rejection of parental and family values.

Part II focuses on teaching and classroom situations. While particularly helpful to teachers, this section will also help parents to understand how middle-grade teaching and learning must differ from that in elementary grades. Chapter 10 clearly defines effective teaching in the middle grades, focusing that agenda for parents and for educators seeking to improve their effectiveness in teaching young adolescents. Caissy's description of how a successful middle-level classroom might look is most helpful. Classroom management issues either unique to, or focused more intensely at, the middle level are clearly described in Chapter 11. Teachers moving to the middle level will find that information particularly helpful and it should help teachers and parents to dispel myths and stereotypes about young adolescents.

Chapter 12 sophisticates the information on intellectual development to a reflective, informative level for middle-grade teachers. Caissy's discussion of thinking-level transition, curriculum issues, lesson planning, and student motivation is excellent. Her treatment of young adolescent "idealism and fantasy" deals with issues that are too frequently overlooked. Chapter 13 combines an extended consideration of physical development with related young adolescent issues, including sex education and substance abuse. The critical impact of social and emotional issues central in teaching young adolescents is described in Chapter 14. Caissy's treatment of peer pressure, stress, and stress management issues is particularly helpful. Chapter 15 discusses the need for teachers to function as referral agents and to help young adolescents get early attention for particular problems they may be facing.

There are few panaceas to anything and this book is not one of them. However, it makes a significant contribution by providing accurate information that can help parents and educators to better understand this most misunderstood of all age groups. Caissy's own understanding of early adolescents and her experience in teaching, studying, and researching them are apparent throughout this book. Her crisply written work should help parents and teachers of young adolescents address their tasks more comfortably, confidently, and successfully.

CONRAD F. TOEPFER, JR., ED.D.

*Professor*
*Department of Learning and Instruction*
*Graduate School of Education*
*State University of New York at Buffalo*
*Buffalo, New York*

# Acknowledgments

Without my former early adolescent students, this book would not have come about. I am indebted to them for fostering my interest in the early adolescent age group. They provided me with the inspiration and motivation (in more ways than one) to try to understand them and to find out what "makes them tick."

To the many researchers in the field of early adolescent development and education whose names are too numerous to mention, I am grateful. Much of this book is based on information they generated through decades of research.

For his assistance during the process of producing the book, I would like to extend my appreciation to my editor, Frank Darmstadt, and others on the staff at Insight Books (including my previous editor, Norma Fox) who made this book possible.

I would also like to express my personal and heartfelt gratitude to Dr. Conrad Toepfer for his careful review of the manuscript and for his valuable suggestions, guidance, wisdom, and inspiration.

For taking the time to thoughtfully review the manuscript, I extend my appreciation to Elizabeth MacDonald and Louise Warner.

I would like to thank my father, John Caissy, and his wife, Wilma, for their support during the writing of this book as well as Elizabeth and Edward Willick, two special early adolescents.

And finally, for his love, support, patience, and assistance during the entire book-writing process, I am most grateful to my husband, Laurence.

# Contents

## II.   TEACHING EARLY ADOLESCENT STUDENTS

# Introduction

Moody, irritable, volatile, smart-mouthed, know-it-all, rebellious, critical, sarcastic, and "too big for their britches." Is there a 10- to 14-year-old child(ren) in your life who fits this description? These are some of the most commonly used words to describe early adolescent children today. Whether you are a parent, teacher, or other person who has contact with early adolescent children, if you would like to know why these children behave the way they do and what early adolescence is all about, this book is for you.

Early adolescents, children aged 10 to 15, are one of the least studied, least understood groups of children in society today. While there are many books available on infant development, early childhood, and the teen years, there are few devoted exclusively to the 10- to 15-year-old child, a child experiencing unprecedented change, growth, and development through the process of puberty. The reason for writing this book is to provide parents, teachers, and others who work with early adolescents with a comprehensive look at early adolescent children, how they think, and why they behave the way they do.

Early adolescence is a unique and significant period in human development. It marks the end of an individual's childhood years and the beginning of youth or young adulthood. It is a time of great transition. For a period of two to four years, during which this transition occurs, early adolescents are in a state of metamorphosis. No longer children, but not yet adults, they are in a world of their own somewhere in between.

At some time during early adolescence, most children will begin or complete the process of puberty. Puberty is the point in human development when sexual maturity begins. The onset of puberty sets into motion the process of sexual development as well as a period of dramatic growth, change, and development in all areas of early adolescent life. There is virtually no aspect of a child's physical, biological, social, emotional, and intellectual development that is not subject to change during these years. And as change occurs in one area, it affects change in the others.

Early adolescent children may gain as much as 50 percent of their adult weight and 25 percent of adult height during puberty. They will become sexually mature. Uneven secretions of hormones in their bodies during the sexual maturation process will cause them to become moody, irritable, and volatile. They will acquire mental skills that will allow them to think more like an adult. With these new skills, they begin to see the world from a whole new perspective. Suddenly, they know it all and adults don't know anything. As they grow more mature, they need to break away from authority figures to develop an identity of their own and become more independent. Rebellion, defiance, and criticism are the results of this process.

Friends take on increasing importance during early adolescence, and peer pressure follows. Insecure in their new world, early adolescents want to look like, dress like, talk like, and act like their friends. As their bodies mature and become more adult-like, they want to act and be like adults but aren't quite sure how to do it. Everything is changing in the early adolescent's world. Everything is new.

Although these are perfectly normal events and behaviors that occur during the early adolescent years, most children are not prepared for them. They don't understand puberty. They don't understand what is happening to them or why it is happening. When they first begin to observe their bodies changing, children often become frightened and alarmed. Why am I growing hair here? Am I getting cancer? Why am I having these funny feelings, and what do they mean? They become extremely self-conscious about their changing bodies, and this leads to anxiety and embarrassment. Worried about what is happening to them, they wonder what will be next. Being an early adolescent isn't easy!

While early adolescents struggle with their development, new behaviors emerge and old ones begin to change. Parents are caught off guard. They begin to struggle with the child's changes and new behaviors and begin to wonder, "Is this the same child I raised all these years?" Once reasonably easy to manage, the child has changed and has become difficult. "Why is he* behaving like this? Why won't she listen to me? What am I doing wrong?" Puzzled and confused by it all, parents ask themselves these questions as they search for reasons for the child's changing behavior and ways. Being a parent of an early adolescent isn't easy!

But nothing is wrong with either the early adolescent child or the parent of the child. What is lacking is a knowledge and understanding of the process of puberty. The child doesn't understand what is happening to him. He is frightened and confused. The parent has long forgotten about the process of puberty and the events and behaviors it entails. Most of all, parents do not associate the many negative behaviors of early adolescent children with the changes the children are experiencing. They do not recognize that early adolescent behavior has little to do with anything the parent has done "wrong."

Student teachers and teachers working with early adolescents for the first time are equally baffled and frustrated by their behaviors. Unpredictable and difficult to manage, early adolescent students are the most challenging of all to work with.

---

*The pronouns *he* and *she* are used interchangeably throughout the book to refer to the early adolescent child. This was done in order to eliminate the need to repeatedly use the terms *he/she* or *they*. Unless otherwise specified, what is said about one sex applies equally to the other.

Puberty is inevitable. It is a natural process and an important part of human development that everyone goes through. There is nothing you can do to stop it. There is nothing you can do to eliminate it. This being the case, it is best to prepare for early adolescence by learning all you can about it, because whether you are a parent, teacher, or other person who has regular contact with early adolescents, the key to working successfully with children during early adolescence is to understand puberty.

The purpose of this book is to provide an understanding of the early adolescent child and early adolescent development. Part I of the book reviews the process of change as it relates to all areas of early adolescent development (physical, biological, emotional, social, and intellectual). Through this part of the book, you have an opportunity to get inside of the early adolescent mind to view things from his or her perspective. This part of the book also outlines the kinds of behavior that can be expected of early adolescents as change occurs in each of the areas, and it presents guidelines and strategies to manage and deal with the behavior of children during these years.

Part II of the book is written for teachers. It examines the early adolescent as a student in the middle-level classroom. From a practical point of view, Part II presents an analysis and review of the impact of early adolescent development (discussed in the first part of the book) on the day-to-day teaching and learning that takes place in the middle-level classroom. Practical ways to deal effectively with early adolescent behavior in the classroom (that is, classroom management and discipline strategies) are provided, as are ways to develop effective lessons and teaching methodologies for students of this age group. Characteristics of successful middle-level teachers and the teacher's role as an adviser and counselor to early adolescent students are also discussed.

This book does not advocate a specific style of parenting or teaching but allows the reader to adopt his or her own style using the information and principles of behavior management provided. The book deals with the growth, development, and behavior of the "average" child. It does not address the more serious or deviant behaviors and problems experienced by some children. The book provides general information only. A physician or psychologist should always be consulted for specific information in specific cases. A list of books that early adolescent children can read to learn about their development is provided, and additional sources of reading for parents, teachers, and other interested adults are also included.

Early adolescents need sympathy and understanding during this period of dramatic change in their lives. This book will prepare you with the information you need to understand the early adolescent child(ren) in your life and enable you to cope successfully with his or her behavior in your role as a parent, teacher, or other caring adult.

# EARLY ADOLESCENT DEVELOPMENT, BEHAVIOR, AND PARENTING

# Physical and Biological Development

Early adolescence is a unique period in human development. It is characterized largely by the dramatic transformation that occurs in children as a result of puberty. Puberty brings about unprecedented physical and biological change in children. These changes strongly affect early adolescent behavior as well as emotional, social, and intellectual development. While all of these areas are interconnected and interrelated, most of the changes that occur in any area of behavior or development can be traced back to physical and biological development, where everything in puberty has its roots. Familiarity with the physical and biological development of early adolescents is necessary before early adolescent behavior and other areas of change and development can be reviewed and understood. Thus, this is where we will begin. In subsequent chapters, we will frequently refer back to the information presented here.

## PUBERTY

The processes involved in the physical growth and sexual development of children during puberty are very complex. Except for a brief period of intrauterine life, at no time in human development do people experience such widespread change, development, and growth. Within a brief period of two to four years, early adolescents develop physically and sexually from children to young adults.

When does puberty begin? The onset of puberty cannot be exactly predicted for each individual child. There is great variability among children in the age of onset of puberty, the rate of development, and the sequence of development once it begins. Two girls (or boys) who are exactly the same chronological age may be in completely different stages of development. There can be differences of 15 to 20 centimeters [cm] (6 to 8 inches) in height and 18 to 27 kilograms [kg] (40 to 60 pounds) in weight between them. Chronological age is therefore a poor predictor of puberty. In most children, however, the process of puberty begins sometime between the ages of 10 and 14, although it can begin as early as 9 and as late as 16 in girls and as early as 9 and as late as 17 in boys.

## FACTORS AFFECTING PUBERTY

How does puberty begin? The timing of the early adolescent growth spurt and sexual development is under the control of the central nervous system in the brain and the endocrine gland system. When puberty begins, the endocrine glands become more active and begin to produce hormones. These hormones are released into the child's body, triggering the initiation of a growth spurt and the beginning of sexual development. While the average child will have this experience between the ages of 10 and 14, the timing seems to depend less on a child's age than on other factors such as his weight or body mass. Researchers have found that when children achieve a certain weight or body mass, the body's metabolism is triggered to increase activity in the endocrine glands, which produce hormones. As these growth hormones are released into the body's bloodstream, sexual development and a growth spurt begin.

Obese and tall children tend to be early developers, while short and thin children tend to develop later. Genetic factors also account for much of the variability in growth and the rate of sexual development. Early or late developers tend to occur in families. Race is another factor that influences the timing of puberty. For example, black children tend to develop earlier than white children.

Nutritional standards also play an important role in determining the rate of growth and the timing of sexual development. Poor nutrition in pregnant mothers or in a developing child's diet can delay or impair growth and sexual development. Chronic malnutrition can delay growth prior to and during early adolescence. This is often seen in Third World countries, where sexual development and the growth spurt begin at a later age in children largely because of poor nutritional standards. Physical and emotional stress as well as poor health standards are other factors that can have a delaying effect.

The endocrine (gland) system is very important in controlling the rate of growth and sexual development in children. The control of the function of the endocrine system is located in the section of the brain called the hypothalamus. The hypothalamus controls the release or suppression of hormones from the pituitary or master gland, which synthesizes and releases various kinds of hormones. These hormones are responsible for controlling the rate of growth and sexual development in early adolescents. The thyroid gland also produces hormones that contribute to this process.

Prior to early adolescence, the physical growth of children is gradual and slow. Each year, a child attains a greater height and weight than in the previous year. This growth, an average of 3.5 to 5 cm ($1\frac{1}{2}$ to 2 inches) a year, is barely noticeable over a long period of time. When puberty begins, however, hormones are produced by the endocrine system and are rapidly and abruptly released into the child's body. This creates a shock to the child's system because it is unfamiliar with the presence of these substances. A temporary chemical imbalance occurs in the child's body as a result of the uneven secretions of hormones. In addition to affecting the growth and sexual development of children, the temporary chemical imbalances are largely responsible for the extremes in emotion, the changes in mood, and the volatility found among early adolescents.

## PUBERTY IN GIRLS

In Western industrialized nations such as the United States, Canada, and Great Britain, the onset of puberty in girls occurs at an average age of 10 to 12 years. The average interval from the initial stages of puberty to menarche (first menstrual period) is about 2 years, with an additional 18 months to 2 years to complete the maturational process.

While there is great variability in the timing and sequence of events of pubertal development, the average girl will complete the overall process over a three- to four-year period. This three- to four-year period involves two stages. During the first 18 months to 2 years (the 10- to 12-year age period), girls experience the initial phases of sexual development and growth (stage one). The first sign of development is usually the appearance of breast buds, followed by a rapidly widening pelvis. This often coincides with, or is rapidly followed by, the appearance of pubic hair, which continues to grow and spread over a larger area for a year or two afterward. Next in the early stage of sexual development is breast enlargement. During this time, the breasts begin to grow rapidly. It is not uncommon for one breast to begin growing before the other or to have both of them growing at an uneven rate. This uneven development, resulting in breasts that are slightly different from each other in size, is temporary. The appearance of axillary (underarm) hair is usually next in the sequence of development. Hair begins to grow in the underarm area and begins to thicken and darken on the legs and arms. During the initial 18-month to 2-year period of development, girls experience the greatest gains they will make in height and weight.

Following this development in stage one, girls then experience menarche or the first menstrual period. This event marks the end of the first stage of development and the beginning of the second (which occurs during the 12- to 14-year age period). The first menstrual periods experienced by girls are usually very irregular because it takes a year or two for the body to adjust to the process of menstruating. Characteristics of menstrual periods in the first year or two following menarche include scanty or excessive bleeding, short or prolonged intervals between periods, periods shorter than five to seven days, or periods longer than five to seven days. Ovulation (the release of a mature egg from the ovary) does not always occur in the early months that follow the first menstrual period. Therefore, fertility may not be present at this time. Cramping and other complaints of discomfort associated with menstruation in a girl who has previously been symptom-free is usually a sign that ovulation has begun. Once ovulation begins, fertility is established.

Children who experience menarche between ages 10 and 12 are considered early developers, those who begin at ages 12 and 13 are considered average, and those who begin at ages 14 or 15 are considered late. However, experiencing menarche at any of these ages is considered normal.

Once menarche has occurred, an additional 18 months to 2 years is needed to complete the sexual maturation process. During this stage, the body becomes more accustomed to the presence of hormones. The process of menstruation and sexual development is refined. The body takes on a more rounded, curvy shape, and hips and thighs become fleshier. The child continues to experience growth in height and weight, although at a slower rate. By the end of the second stage, approximately three to four years have passed. At this point, the child will have achieved most of her full adult height and will be sexually mature. The average gain in height over the three- to four-year period for girls is about 5 to 10 cm (2 to 4 inches) per year, while the average gain in weight is 3 to 5.5 kg (6 to 12 pounds) per year.

## PUBERTY IN BOYS

The onset of puberty in boys is about two years behind that of girls. On average, the male growth spurt begins sometime between the ages of 12 and 14, with an average of four years in total to complete the overall process. The initial phases of development include the appearance of pubic hair and enlargement of the reproductive organs or genitals. As the reproductive organs continue to grow and develop, boys experience the growth of axillary (underarm) hair. This is followed by growth of hair on the face, upper lip, legs, and abdomen. Hair on the chin does not usually appear until genitals are fully developed. Thus, it is considered one of the last phases of development. During this four-year period, boys make tremendous gains in height and weight. An average of 7 to 10 cm (3 to 4 inches) per year in height and 4.5 to 9 kg (10 to 20 pounds) in weight is normal. As this growth occurs, the body takes on increasingly muscular form.

In Western industrialized countries, the average 13-year-old boy and girl are about the same size. But whereas girls' growth and development is largely on the decline, boys are just beginning their growth spurt. By the age of 16 or 17, the development of both sexes is usually complete.

## CHANGES IN BODY FUNCTION
## AND APPEARANCE

During puberty, both boys and girls experience various changes in body function and appearance, in addition to the process of sexual development discussed thus far. These occur as a result of endocrine gland activity at some time during the four-year interval.

First, oil glands become more active during puberty and produce excessive amounts of sebum, an oily substance secreted by tiny glands on the outer layer of the skin. Skin becomes more oily as a result. For 80 percent of early adolescents, this leads to skin problems, the most common being acne. As the pores of the skin fill up with oil, they can become blocked, causing pimples and blackheads.

Because of the production of excess oil and sweat, hair becomes more oily and requires more frequent washing. Once again, as the child matures and hormone and oil gland production becomes more stable, these problems tend to decline or disappear.

Perspiration is also experienced by early adolescents as sweat glands become more active. As children begin to perspire more heavily, body odor, especially from under the arms and feet, results.

Some young people develop stretch marks during the growth spurt. These are purplish or white lines that appear on the skin, commonly on the hips or buttocks. They occur because skin is stretched too much during rapid growth, and it loses its elasticity as a result. These marks will usually fade or become less noticeable with the passage of time.

Voice changes also occur in both boys and girls during early adolescence, although these changes are most noticeable in boys. Voices in both sexes become lower in pitch and more adult-like in sound. During the growth spurt, most boys will experience a cracking or squeaking in their voices as they attempt to change pitch. This can last from a few months to a year until the vocal chords are fully developed.

## VARIATIONS IN DEVELOPMENT

Having reviewed the process of sexual development that early adolescents experience, it is important to emphasize that the rate and sequence of growth and development can vary greatly from child to child. The process presented here represents only the most common sequence or average length of time involved. These terms can be misleading because there can be many significant variations from the given sequences and timing of development, and these variations are considered perfectly normal. For example, increased perspiration and the growth of underarm hair may be the first signs that puberty is beginning for a boy rather than the processes mentioned previously. Girls may experience menarche before the breast enlargement phase or may not experience the growth of underarm hair until after the first menstrual period. Whereas one girl may have experienced her first period by the age of 11, another may not do so until age 15. Whereas some boys will experience a gradual increase in height and weight over a four-year period, others may make most of these gains in only 18 months. Variation is common and normal. However, although problems are unlikely, children who begin development outside the average range of 10 to 14 years should be examined by a physician in the event that there may be some abnormality. In fact, when in doubt about any of the change processes in puberty, it is best to consult a physician. While serious problems are rare, if they do exist, they can often be remedied by medical intervention and medication.

## PROBLEMS WITH SEXUAL DEVELOPMENT

Problems with sexual development during puberty are found more frequently in girls. Some of the most common problems for which parents seek advice are as follows. In females, the most common problem is irregularity of menstrual cycles. Excessive bleeding, prolonged intervals between periods, scanty bleeding, and periods occurring more frequently than once a month are common complaints. On average, 12 to 18 months must pass after the onset of menstruation before regular, predictable menstrual periods of five to seven days in length at 26- to 30-day intervals are established. While this is the case for the majority of girls, some never experience periods that are regular and predictable.

In boys, the most common problem appears to be breast enlargement (gynecomastia). This occurs in almost all early adolescent males and is rarely serious. Slight to modest enlargement of the breast occurs as a result of hormonal development. The problem usually resolves itself with the passage of time (about a year to 18 months on average).

## EARLIER ONSET OF PUBERTY OVER TIME

People who have worked with early adolescents over a long period of time (for example, teachers), often make the comment that sexual development in girls seems to be occurring earlier and earlier as time goes by. While such observations may seem imaginary, there is scientific evidence to suggest that this in fact is happening, although not as dramatically as one might be led to believe. There has been a decline in the average age of menarche over the last century in the United States and western European countries. Studies demonstrate that in these countries, the average age of menarche has declined an average of 3.5 months per decade since the mid-1800s. In 1960, the average age of menarche was 13. Today it is 12.

The earlier onset of puberty in both boys and girls over time can be attributed to several factors, the most important being improved diets and nutritional standards as well as better health care. Diet additives (hormones) given to livestock to bring about earlier maturation and a rapid increase in the animal's weight have also been implicated. It is thought that the additives are passed along to the developing child through consumption of meat that contains these additives.

The decline in the average age of puberty has been slowing down in recent decades and is now showing signs of abatement. Researchers believe this is attributable to the fact that almost optimum nutritional and health standards have been achieved in Western industrialized nations today. It is interesting to note that although the average age of menarche has dropped over the last century, the earliest age at which menarche is possible (about 9 years of age) has remained the same over time. Thus, there is no need to fear that toddlers will soon skip childhood and go right into puberty! There is also similar evidence that children have been becoming taller by an average of 1 to 3 cm (half an inch to an inch) per decade since studies began in this area in 1900.

## PHYSICAL GROWTH AND DEVELOPMENT

While we have focused on the development of sexual characteristics thus far, the release of hormones into the body has a significant effect on other aspects of physical growth and development of a child. Although bone and skeletal tissue develop and expand with the gain in height and weight during puberty, the body does not develop as a whole. Rather than experiencing gradual and equal growth in all parts of the body as in childhood, different parts of the body experience growth at different times, resulting in the appearance of disproportionate body parts. This usually follows a set sequence. The outer extremities (hands and feet) develop first, then the arms and legs. These are followed by development in hip width and chest breadth. Shoulder breadth follows. Finally, the trunk lengthens and chest depth is established. The growth of the body segments usually occurs at four-month intervals. Boys generally complete their physical development and achieve maximum height sometime around the age of 17, while girls do so around the age of 15.

During the period of rapid physical development, bone growth surpasses muscle development. As a result, bones lack the protection of muscles and the support of tendons. It is this uneven bone-muscle growth that causes poor physical coordination and the awkwardness characteristic of early adolescents. Hardening (ossification) of cartilage in the skeleton makes sitting on hard chairs uncomfortable for these young people and causes the syndrome commonly referred to as "ants in the pants."

Changes also occur in the cardiovascular and respiratory systems. Lungs increase in size. The weight of the heart nearly doubles. However, the size and tension of the arteries that carry blood to and from the heart do not expand rapidly enough to accommodate its greater pumping capacity. Blood pressure increases as a result.

Differences in the rate of growth of body parts are so varied and great during early adolescence that almost every part of the body is affected, even the lens of the eye. Temporary myopia (short-sightedness) may be experienced for a few months until the lens of the eye adjusts to rapid physical growth and change.

Extreme restlessness and alternating periods of seemingly limitless energy and total fatigue are common during early adolescence. This results from variations in the body's metabolism. At times, early adolescents may go for hours without any need for sleep, while at other times, they sleep for inordinately long periods. During a period of rapid physical growth, the body works overtime. Overexertion in physical activity during this time can result in chronic fatigue.

During early adolescence, dietary requirements are altered by body growth and changes in metabolism. During the growth spurt, the stomach becomes elongated and attains a greater capacity. Coupled with the need for more food to accommodate rapid physical growth, this often results in a tremendous increase in appetite. As a general rule, the caloric needs of the average developing early adolescent male or female (aged 10 to 14) are equivalent to those of the average adult male or female (aged 23 to 50). Good nutrition during this period is essential to healthy physical development. Unfortunately, good nutrition is not always a priority in the lives of most early adolescents.

# The Impact of
# Physical Development
# on Early Adolescents

Having reviewed the processes of growth and sexual development as they occur during early adolescence, we now turn to an examination of the impact of this development on the behavior of early adolescent children.

## EARLY ADOLESCENTS'
## REACTION TO PUBERTY

As sexual development and the growth spurt begin, most children are unaware of what is happening to them or why it is happening. Thus, they are caught off guard when it begins. As far as they are concerned, they are children and have been for as long as they can remember. While they are aware that they have grown taller and heavier over time, their body characteristics have essentially remained the same. Then one day, for no reason apparent to them, things begin to change. Suddenly, there is pubic hair where there was none before. They begin to ask themselves questions such as "Do I have a disease? Why is there hair here? Should I tell anyone about it? Is anyone going to notice and laugh at me? Is something bad going to happen to me? Do I have cancer? Why is this happening?" Body odor resulting from activated sweat glands can lead to peers calling a child names (for example, smelly, stinky, and worse!). The child doesn't realize that he has begun the process of sexual development, let alone that the odor from his sweat glands has become offensive to others as a result. For many children, the onset of puberty is a frightening experience.

Without intervention, most early adolescents do not make the connection mentally that their bodies are changing as a result of growth and sexual development. They know that they are kids, and kids don't have pubic hair or breasts. So they conclude that something must be "wrong" with them.

## EDUCATING EARLY ADOLESCENTS ABOUT PUBERTY

As they attempt to figure out what is going on in their bodies, early adolescents wonder whether people notice the changes. They also worry about what others will think if they do notice the changes. It is important, therefore, that early adolescents be prepared for puberty. They should understand the processes that they will experience as well as how they can expect to feel about the changes that result. While this may not make the physical changes feel any more comfortable, it can be of significant help psychologically. Understanding the process of puberty can remove a great deal of fear and anxiety associated with sexual development. Thus, parents need to talk to their children about puberty before it begins or when they recognize that the initial stages have begun. They need to explain to a child that her body will be undergoing a transformation over the next few years as she changes from being a child to a young adult. Things to be expected at various stages should be reviewed, and the child should be reassured that the process is perfectly normal and natural.

Once puberty begins, parents can further discuss characteristics of the specific phase the child is in, while continually reassuring the child that what he is experiencing is normal. As a parent, you might point out that you went through this process yourself at one time, and you may want to discuss how you felt about it. Encourage your child to come to you if she has any questions or concerns about her development or if she needs help in coping with it. It is also a good idea to give the child more information than what he is specifically asking about because children are often reluctant to ask too many questions on this subject. Try to anticipate a child's questions and provide as much information as possible, while on the topic.

Some parents are not comfortable talking to their children about growth and sexual development. If this is the case, parents may seek the help of other adults qualified to speak on the topic (for example, a school nurse or a relative). This is especially helpful to a single male parent of a daughter or a single female parent of a son.

There are also several books written for children to read about their changing bodies. Suggested books for this purpose are listed at the end of this book. Parents can provide these books for their children to read as a means of educating the child. This should be done when parents feel the time is appropriate, that is, when a child is mature enough to handle it or appears to be in the beginning stages of puberty. Once the child has read the book(s), the parent can encourage the child to ask any questions she may have, or the parent can make herself available to discuss the material further, if desired. Children may not always be comfortable asking questions or discussing the material. Nonetheless, they should get information from a reliable source so that they are aware of factual information. Sometimes children of this age rely on their peers for information. Of course, in these circumstances, they can receive a great deal of misinformation because peers are not likely to be highly informed on the subject themselves.

The book(s) provided for the child need not be handed to the child with instructions to have it read by a certain time, although this approach works well for some. Other parents like to read the book(s) together with the child. Another more indirect approach preferred by some parents is to obtain a suitable book and put it on the coffee table or in the child's room with more indirect instructions such as, "I was in the library (or book store) today, Jenny, and I picked up a book that I think you should read. You are getting older now, and soon your body will begin changing as you become a teenager and an adult. I would like you to read this book when you get a chance because it explains what the body changes are all about. Then maybe after you've read the book, we can talk about it for a while if you want to." You can be assured that the child's curiosity will motivate her to read it, particularly if puberty has already begun. Many parents report that the child finished reading the book the very same day!

These are just a few suggestions as to how to approach and address the issue with your child. The approach you choose should be one that is most appropriate for you and your situation. Whether you choose to address the subject directly, by speaking to the child about it yourself, or indirectly, by having him speak to others or read about it, the child should be assured about several things.

First, it is important to stress that puberty is a natural and perfectly normal process, and that every person has to go through it to become an adult. All of your relatives and friends and even you, the child's parent, went through puberty. It is necessary to keep reassuring the child that all the changes he or she is experiencing during puberty are normal. Individual early adolescents often feel that they are the only ones undergoing change. Although it is obvious to the adults around them, early adolescents don't always recognize or acknowledge that their peers are changing too. At this age, they are still self-centered and thus are very self-conscious and embarrassed about their development. What is obvious to you may not be obvious to them. As a result, they can feel very alone during the process.

Another important thing to stress when talking about changes to early adolescents is that although the physical changes may be a bit uncomfortable at times, they don't hurt or cause great pain. By associating bleeding with a cut or pain, for example, young girls can develop the same mental picture when they think about the menstrual process. Early adolescents also need to be reassured that nothing "bad" is going to happen to them as a result of the changes. For example, as they experience changes in their voices, some boys fear that they will lose them completely. Some girls fear that when they menstruate, all of their blood will come out and they will bleed to death. Remember, these are children, and they think differently than adults.

Great differences in the timing and sequence of events in puberty cause many unnecessary fears for early adolescents. If they are in any way out of step in their development with their closest friends or peers (and there is a high probability they will be), they begin to worry or panic. They think something is wrong with them because they don't appear to be the same as everyone else. In their perception, "everyone else" could be a few students or a classroom full. Thus it is important to emphasize that although everyone goes through puberty, each person is different and will go through the changes in his own way, at his own pace, and in his own time.

## GIVING EARLY OR LATE MATURERS ADDITIONAL REASSURANCE

While some anxiety about the pace of development between herself and her peers is normal for any early adolescent, it can be especially problematic for early or late maturers. Early maturers worry about why they are developing while none of their peers are doing so. They are very self-conscious and embarrassed about outward signs of change. Girls developing breasts ahead of their peers will often try to conceal them by wearing loose tops or baggy clothing. They may even wear vests or coats and heavy jackets in school when there is no need for it. Some early developers even go so far as to wrap cloth bandages around their chests so that they will look flat and not show any sign of development. Boys will often tease an early developing girl about her "boobies," causing her great embarrassment. If a girl develops dark hair on her legs before her peers, she may insist on wearing pants every day to cover them up.

While early maturers often endure embarrassment and self-consciousness initially, their self-confidence and self-esteem are held intact in the long run. Because they look older than their peers, they are usually treated more as adults by other people and are often admired by their peers for this reason.

Late maturers, however, seem to suffer psychologically more than any other group of early adolescent individuals. Feelings of great anxiety set in as they observe their friends and peers around them undergoing physical changes or becoming fully developed. These individuals are frequently laughed at or ridiculed by their peers because they don't match up physically. Because late maturers don't recognize themselves as such, they begin to feel something is wrong with them. This generates feelings of insecurity and inferiority and results in a lack of self-confidence. Being constantly ridiculed by their peers for something over which they have no control becomes almost unbearable for some, and it can have negative and sometimes devastating effects on many areas of their lives such as school grades, social life, and health. For example, Brent was a 15-year-old school boy who was lagging behind his peers developmentally. Brent dreaded going to physical education classes because while he and his classmates changed into their gym clothes, some of them would make fun of his undeveloped genitals. Math class preceded physical education in Brent's daily schedule. Brent had always been an "A" student in math, but his grades began dropping dramatically with no logical explanation. After much thought and investigation, the teacher discovered that Brent was the butt of jokes during his physical education class because he was so short and undeveloped. The teacher learned that Brent's poor math performance was not due to any lack of ability on his part. It was instead due to the fact that Brent spent most of his time in math class thinking about what was going to happen in the gym class that followed. He worried about being ridiculed and laughed at and about what he would say or do this time. He so worried about his next class that he wasn't listening to the teacher and thus couldn't perform well. His grades went down as a result.

Early and especially late maturers need constant reassurance and support from their parents that they are normal, and that they are simply developing behind (or ahead of) their peers and will soon catch up. They should be encouraged to be patient and wait just a little longer. If the child continues to doubt that he will ever begin development, ask him to look around in his environment to see if he can find any undeveloped adults. Parents who have experienced late development themselves and had similar anxieties in their youth can also relate these stories as a form of encouragement and support for the child.

## DIFFICULTIES ADJUSTING TO PHYSICAL CHANGE

While adjusting psychologically to the changes that puberty brings is difficult, early adolescents may also have difficulty adapting physically to ongoing changes in their bodies, once the process begins. This is particularly evident in any type of athletic activity. A child who has grown accustomed to achieving certain results through certain physical actions finds that during the growth spurt, the same actions can produce completely different results. For example, because of increased arm and leg growth, a boy may have finally adjusted his method of throwing a ball to achieve the best results. He no sooner masters this skill when he is again thrown off balance by the onset of the next growth level: hip width and chest breadth. So he is forced to adjust his technique once again. Because early adolescents seldom recognize or attribute their physical coordination problems to the fact that their bodies are undergoing rapid change, they become extremely frustrated with themselves and their inability to perform certain tasks and skills, especially those that they feel they have mastered. This is an ongoing problem that lasts from several months to several years, or until the growth process is complete. Growth is usually complete at age 15 for girls and at age 17 for boys.

For this reason, participation in competitive sports should be temporarily downplayed or discouraged during the growth spurt. Fully developed individuals have a great advantage physically and thus perform well. However, those still in the early developmental stages or those who have not yet begun development are at a disadvantage. These children become very frustrated when they have to compete with others much bigger, stronger, and more skilled than themselves. Competitive sports among early adolescents can be very frustrating and unfair to late maturers who feel inadequate when they are never chosen to be on sports teams or are always chosen last. Moreover, their lack of ability or awkwardness can draw undue and embarrassing ridicule from classmates. For example, Jerry is standing around with other classmates waiting to be chosen for a baseball team. Classmates call up to the team leader, "Don't pick Jerry; he's a weakling. He always drops the ball." Or "Don't pick Patti. She can't hit a thing." Or imagine being Andrew, who is always picked last. Classmates don't want him on their basketball team because he is too short to shoot baskets or dribble the ball successfully. Unfortunately, comments such as these take a toll on the self-confidence of these late developers. Many of them begin to believe that they are no good or that they can't do anything. While competitive sports and activities should be discouraged, those that involve self-competition (for example, running or push-ups) should be encouraged during the growth spurt years, in moderation. Early adolescents can then compete with themselves, trying to better their own skills rather than competing with others who have significant advantages over them.

Physical activity is necessary during early adolescence for all of the usual health-oriented reasons, but also because it provides a good outlet for the excessive restlessness that characterizes children of this age group. With the heart and arteries developing more slowly than the growth rate of other body parts, for a period of time, the heart cannot pump blood fast enough throughout the body to accommodate the needs of an energetic early adolescent. Therefore, moderation in physical exercise is advised until the heart and arteries are fully developed. Overtaxing the system during this growth stage can lead to medical problems.

As well as overall physical coordination, fine-motor skills are also temporarily affected by rapid growth. Children may experience frustration or difficulty with sewing, and constructing models, playing instruments, or learning to type—basically, with any activities requiring the use of precision with their hands.

For a time during their development, the everyday movements of early adolescents may be clumsy and awkward, causing them much embarrassment. Examples of this behavior include tripping over things as their feet grow larger, spilling things at the dinner table, or bumping chairs or tables as they rise to get up.

Because of rapid growth in height and weight, early adolescents will not stay with one shoe or clothing size for long. Shoes or clothes that fit one month may be too small the next. Also, early adolescents may have trouble finding clothes that fit them well during any part of the growth spurt as a result of the uneven rate of growth of different body parts. For example, the sleeves of a child's shirt may be too long when it is purchased but might be perfect in a few months. The waist may be too long in a girl's dress when it is purchased, but a few months later, it may fit just fine. Shoes may be worn for only a few months before they become too small. Parents should be aware of this situation in making their decisions to purchase clothing for their children during the growth spurt years. To avoid additional expense, many parents buy fewer clothes for their children during this two-year period, knowing that the children will outgrow them quickly. Others buy clothing slightly larger than the children need so that they will get a longer period of wear out of them. This is particularly helpful when buying coats, jackets, and other seasonal items. A winter coat, for example, is a significant expense, and during the growth spurt years, the child will likely get only one year of wear out of it.

That represents a significant outlay of money for an item that may be worn for only three or four months.

## DIETARY PATTERNS

During early adolescence, dietary requirements are altered by body growth and changes in metabolism. Good nutrition, of course, is essential to healthy physical development, and so a nutritious diet (one recommended by the government's national food guide) should be stressed. It is ironic, however, that at a time in their lives when nutrition is so important, early adolescents often overindulge in large quantities of poorly selected "junk" foods or those that have little nutritional value. While this is to be discouraged to the extent possible, it is a normal experimental activity of this age group.

At some time during early adolescence, girls may become preoccupied with various types of diets in their quest to look like the latest media star. While short-term experimentation can be relatively harmless, it can have a negative effect on body development and can lead to eating disorders such as anorexia nervosa if carried out over prolonged periods. Anorexia nervosa is a complex, life-threatening mental illness in which the victim has an intense fear of becoming fat and, as a result, pursues slimness through self-starvation, even unto death. Reported cases of this disease have increased tremendously in recent years. While the disease may or may not be diagnosed in early adolescence, it almost always has its roots in the early adolescent growth years.

During the early adolescent growth spurt, the stomach becomes elongated and attains a greater capacity. This coupled with the need for more food to accommodate rapid physical growth often results in a tremendous increase in appetite. Early adolescents can develop ravenous appetites that often astound their parents, who feel that they are feeding a bottomless pit at times. However, this is a temporary situation that improves or passes once full growth is achieved and stabilized.

## SELF-CONSCIOUSNESS ABOUT
## PHYSICAL CHANGES

During early adolescence, children feel self-conscious about the physical changes they experience related to growth and hormone production. These include acne, perspiration, voice changes, and the growth of axillary hair, among others. Children can also become extremely sensitive about any body traits that are unique to themselves. These include moles or birthmarks as well as any body part that deviates even slightly from the norm (for example, big nose, big ears, bushy eyebrows). Because of their extreme self-consciousness about these things, it is important to be sensitive to the feelings of early adolescents and to avoid making fun of, or joking about, any of their changing physical traits. They need to be reassured that just because they have a particular body trait doesn't make them any less of a person. They might be told that inside qualities count more than outward appearances. To illustrate this point, parents might ask a child if he would rather have a friend who is not very good-looking but who is nice, shares things, is sensitive to his feelings, is loyal, and so on as opposed to having a friend who is good-looking on the outside but who doesn't treat him well, is not reliable, and so on. It can be emphasized that no one is perfect and that very few people are near perfect in their looks. Even when these near-perfect people (models) are asked about their looks, they point out that they have some traits or flaws they would rather not have.

Because early adolescents become extremely modest about their changing bodies, they are reluctant to allow anyone to see them. Thus they prefer to change their clothes in complete privacy and to keep their private belongings and clothes (for example, bras, deodorant) in places that are their own and that others do not have access to. Because of their modesty, early adolescents, especially girls, are reluctant to go to a physician's office for any type of physical examination, especially if the physician is of the opposite sex.

# Emotional Development

Emotions common to the early adolescent age group are many and varied. They can best be described as unstable, unpredictable, and extreme. The everyday emotions early adolescents experience are related to biological development as well as to problems they experience adjusting mentally to the process of growing up and becoming sexually and physically mature. The release of various hormones into the body at uneven rates during puberty causes temporary chemical imbalances. These imbalances are largely responsible for the characteristic stormy emotions of early adolescents.

## MOODINESS

As the body attempts to adjust to the presence of increasing amounts of hormones, the uneven secretions affect the emotions of early adolescents, causing them to be unstable. The most obvious outward expression of unstable emotional activity is moodiness and mood swings. A child who appears very happy and content one hour may be miserable the next, sometimes because of some seemingly insignificant event, at other times for no apparent reason. Frequent changes in mood are often accompanied by giggling, laughter, pouting, or intense anger.

Early adolescents experience tremendous fluctuations in their emotions. The highs are very high, and the lows are very low. Individual emotional responses to situations are often out of proportion to the event. Early adolescents can become very upset, showing excessive anger and tears for a very trivial reason. At other times, when getting angry or emotional is justified, they underreact, showing little or no emotion. Early adolescents can also hide their emotions well when they choose to. They often react nonchalantly to an event that may be upsetting them. For example, as a parent is scolding a child, the child may stand cold-faced, showing no emotion and appearing as if he is not absorbing the message. It may appear as if the parent's message is going in one ear and out of the other. While sometimes this is the case, many times the child is listening but is hurt or emotionally upset and does not want to show or admit it to the parent. As a result, the child hides his emotions or shows no emotion at all.

Because of their emotional highs and lows and because early adolescents can hide their feelings, their emotions can be easily misjudged at times. For example, Emily accompanied her parents on a vacation to a northern wilderness resort. She did not want to go with her parents because she thought it would be boring. Before they went, she protested vehemently against going. Then, when they got there, Emily's mother observed her daughter acting with indifference for most of the time they were there. Emily gave the impression that she was not having a good time. After they returned home, Emily's mother was surprised when she overheard Emily talking to her friend on the telephone about the great time she had up north. She talked about how much fun it was to go for boat rides on the lake with her father, how they fed the wildlife, and how she had read two new books while they were there. Because Emily originally did not want to go on the trip, she couldn't admit to her mother that she was having a better time than she expected. So, Emily acted bored and indifferent when she really wasn't feeling that way at all.

During periods of moodiness, early adolescents can be rude or sarcastic. While at times it is intentional, early adolescents usually are so focused on themselves and their needs, they do not realize that they are being rude or that they are hurting other people's feelings. For example, when John's uncle came to visit, John's father called up to his bedroom saying, "John, Uncle Bill is here and wants to see you and talk to you for a little while." John replied within hearing range of Uncle Bill, "I don't want to talk to him right now. I'm listening to my favorite song on the radio." This was, no doubt, an embarrassing situation for both John's father and Uncle Bill.

Early adolescents often ignore adult guests who arrive at their parents' home or don't acknowledge that they are there. They may stay in their bedrooms for long periods of time after the guests arrive, and when they do come out, they may say nothing to acknowledge the guest's presence. As Cheryl passes through the room where her parents' guests are sitting, her mother says, "Cheryl, Mr. and Mrs. Smith are here visiting us. Aren't you going to say hello?" to which Cheryl responds, "Oh, hello," and then rushes off to another room without further conversation. This behavior embarrasses parents who are certain their guests will conclude they are bringing up rude and thoughtless children.

## ANGER

Anger is another common emotion expressed by early adolescents. It is most often triggered by the frustrations early adolescents feel as a result of growing up and learning what life is all about. The most characteristic method of showing anger is to leave the situation and make a scene in doing so (for example, storming out of rooms, slamming doors). Situations that especially precipitate anger among early adolescents include unfairness (the child's perception of unfairness), the "borrowing" or taking of their belongings by siblings, infringement of their private living areas (people "snooping" in their bedrooms), teasing (especially about their appearance), being talked about by others, and things not going their way.

Early adolescent anger is often expressed in sudden, furious outbursts. Children commonly release their emotions and anger on those who have nothing to do with the cause (for example, teachers, parents, siblings). For example, in an emotional outburst, Edward tells his teacher that a homework assignment is stupid when he is really venting his frustration because a classmate just made fun of his new haircut. Having just arrived at the dinner table, Jane comments to her mother, "Spaghetti again? I'm sick of having spaghetti. We always have spaghetti. Can't you ever make anything else?" Her mother, in fact, may not have made spaghetti for several weeks. Jane, however, just had a disagreement with her best friend over the phone and is releasing her anger on her mother rather than on the friend who is responsible for making her angry. Because of the importance of friendships in their lives, early adolescents are hesitant to vent their anger and frustration on their peers. It is also easier for early adolescents to vent their anger elsewhere than it is to confront the source of their anger or the problem. At times, they are not even aware of what the source is. Siblings are among the most common targets of early adolescent frustration and anger. Fighting and arguing with brothers and sisters is common as a result.

Early adolescents eventually realize that losing control of their emotions and lashing out irrationally, especially in front of their peers, is not as easily accepted as it was during childhood. As a result, early adolescents eventually learn to control and express their feelings in a socially acceptable way. Appropriate reactions are often determined by observing what adults do in similar situations, as well as how characters on television and in the media respond in similar circumstances.

## FEARS, WORRIES, AND ANXIETY

Early adolescents have many fears and worries. These fears, both real and imagined, are frequent. Fears are no longer those of childhood but are related to various social situations and what might happen in these situations. For example, early adolescents worry a lot about their physical appearance—having stylish clothes or a fashionable haircut is important to them. As a result, early adolescents spend inordinate amounts of time deciding what they should wear to school or any social event and then worry about whether they made the "right" choice. This is determined by whether they draw compliments from their peers ("Everyone loved my new pants"), ridicule ("Everyone laughed at my new pants"), or indifference ("No one noticed my new pants").

Early adolescents also worry about school. While they may worry about passing and doing well academically, more often they worry about the social aspects of school. How to act with others in a more adult-like fashion and particularly how to act with members of the opposite sex are some of the worries typical of this age group. For example, Patrick thinks, "Wow, I think Isabel likes me. Now what do I do? Or Laura thinks, "What if he comes over here to talk to me? I'll die! What should I say?"

Anxiety is another common emotion of this age group and is closely related to fear and worry. Undue anxiety may be generated about almost anything, but commonly about physical development, such as lack of size, lack of sexual development, lack of muscular strength, obesity, acne, perspiration, and many of the other examples of physical change we have already discussed.

Anxiety is also generated as a result of differences in the ages at which puberty begins in boys and girls. In childhood, males are generally larger and stronger than girls, whereas during puberty, girls develop more quickly and become the larger and stronger of the two sexes. Not recognizing this as a temporary situation, boys are embarrassed because they are suddenly shorter and weaker than girls just at a time in their lives when they have convinced themselves that they are physically superior. Girls who mature earlier than boys develop more mature interests and want to share them with boys who are not yet ready. Rejecting the "immature" attitudes of their male age mates, they begin to look to older boys for friendship.

One trait of early adolescents that causes them much anxiety is their tendency to worry about what other people (especially peers) think of them. This includes what people think about the way they dress, the way they act, what they say, how they look, and so on. This anxiety stems from their lack of self-confidence and insecurity during the early adolescent years when they are struggling to discover who they are and experimenting with various roles in the process. The most worrisome years for early adolescents are during the ages of 13 and 14.

## INSTABILITY

Instability is another characteristic of early adolescents. It can apply to their emotional state as well as to their interests and goals, which seem to be constantly changing. One minute they engage themselves in an activity with great fervor; the next minute they abandon it and declare that they hate it. This does not minimize the seriousness of their interest or the project involved. At the time it was undertaken, their intentions were good and they enjoyed it. However, things can change quite quickly. For example, Sean decided that he wanted to learn to play the guitar. He could hardly wait. He read about guitars and spent weeks convincing his parents to buy a guitar and pay for guitar lessons. They bought the guitar and paid for his lessons. Six months later, he no longer had an interest in the guitar or guitar lessons. In another example, Elizabeth tells her mother that she loves pink, and she wants pink clothes for her upcoming birthday. Her mother passes the word around to relatives who inquire about what type of birthday gift they might buy for Elizabeth. When her birthday arrives a few weeks later, Elizabeth is disappointed because many of her gifts are pink and now she likes purple.

Because of instability, decisions early adolescents make today are changed tomorrow, and adults don't know how to cope with it. For example, Anne's mother found her in tears one afternoon because her best friend, Lisa, had lied to her. Anne declares that she hates Lisa and never wants to see her again. Anne's mother sympathizes with her and consoles her and is then surprised to see Anne and Lisa going shopping together the next day.

## EXTREMES

Along with extremes in emotions during early adolescence comes the use of extremes in vocabulary. Early adolescents commonly describe items or events, especially those that are important to them, using a vocabulary of extremes. For example, "I love this or I hate that. This book was excellent. Those pants are horrible. Everybody was there." They also tend to describe things or events in dramatic fashion, sometimes exaggerating them all out of proportion. Adults see this as "making mountains out of mole hills."

## ACCEPTING THEIR NEW BODIES

One of the most difficult tasks early adolescents face is the acceptance of the physical and biological changes taking place within their bodies. All early adolescents experience discomfort with this process, but those not educated about the changes experience the most discomfort, self-consciousness, and frustration when the changes begin. Compounding this is the fact that the onset of puberty, as well as the rate of physical development during puberty, varies significantly from child to child, and there are no set standards that early adolescents can refer to that would indicate where they should be at a particular time in their development.

As early adolescents begin to realize that their bodies are taking on adult form, they worry about how they will turn out and what they will look like. As they grow up, children develop a vision of what they think they will look like when they become adults. While children are aware to some degree that they look like their fathers or mothers, they do not consider genetics in their thinking about how they will look someday. Rather than consider that they will inherit most of their traits from their parents, they form visions of what their physical appearance should be like from culturally determined norms. These include stereotypes of masculinity and femininity portrayed in the media. Early adolescents want to look, dress, and act like fashion models in magazine advertisements; actors, actresses, and singers on television, in videos, and in movies; and sports celebrities. The emphasis in the media on beauty and sexiness reinforces stereotypes even further. Boys identify strongly with the "masculine" look: height, shoulder width, and a well-proportioned physique. Girls are concerned with hips, breasts, legs, and waists.

As the early adolescent child develops, she compares her appearance and body to these ideals. She quickly discovers that her body is not turning out to be the vision she had in her mind, and she is very disappointed. As a result, she becomes very sensitive and self-conscious about her appearance and body not being perfect.

Early adolescents tend not to focus on the positive aspects of their appearance and development, but rather dwell on the negative. Becoming critical of themselves, they identify minor flaws in their appearance and exaggerate them all out of proportion. At times, through adult eyes, the flaws may not even exist. To the child, however, these flaws are very real and a source of great anxiety. Examples are, "I have the biggest hips/ears/feet in the whole world. This pimple is so ugly that I couldn't possibly go out today. The mole on my shoulder is the ugliest thing I've ever seen. I can't go to the beach because everyone will stare at it."

Even though they realize that they aren't becoming the idealized vision they had imagined, they try all the harder to make themselves look that way. Believing that certain advertised products will help them change their looks is one way of dealing with this. Wanting to look like the media ideal, early adolescents, especially girls, set about unrealistically trying to change their appearance to match the media model as closely as possible. For example, girls will try a variety of diets to keep slim ("so I won't be fat"), try various exercise programs ("to get rid of my big hips"), use excessive amounts of deodorant ("so I won't smell"), use excessive amounts of acne medication ("to get rid of my horrible pimples"), and take excessive numbers of baths and showers ("so I won't have B.O. and greasy hair"). They also fuss incessantly with their hair, believing that they need a large number of hair care products to manage it. This is so that the hair looks perfect all the time, just as it does on women in the television commercials.

While obsessions with personal appearance usually don't appear in the early stages of puberty, they become more pronounced as time goes on. It is not unusual for a child who has hated baths, hated washing her hair, and hated changing into clean clothes to reverse this thinking almost overnight. While these obsessions with personal cleanliness and appearance carry on through most of the teen years, they generally subside once the child has completed his or her physical development and has fully accepted and adjusted to his or her body image.

## INFERIORITY

Unfortunately, early adolescent development and appearance are related to self-esteem (that is, how good or bad a person feels about himself or herself). Feelings of inferiority are common during early adolescence and are tied to a general lack of self-confidence, insecurity, and low self-esteem. While there are many reasons why early adolescents develop feelings of inferiority, one of the main causes is unattractiveness, whether real or perceived. If children think they are unattractive, they feel that they aren't as good as those who are and that people won't like them as well as a result. Another reason for feeling inferior is having few or no friends. When this happens, a child concludes that because nobody likes him, he must not be as good as other kids. He feels like a loser or a failure, and he may become depressed. Perceiving oneself as unintelligent is another common reason for feeling inferior. Early adolescents think that if they aren't "smart," they aren't as good as others. When other kids call them names, such as "dummy," it further reinforces the feelings of inferiority they already have.

Early adolescents who are at an advantage are those who are

attractive and closely meet cultural norms. They are usually admired by their peers, are popular, and have a positive self-concept as a result. For children who least meet the qualities of the idealized norm, the opposite can be true. Overweight children and those who have not yet developed, for example, are often ignored by peers, enjoy less popularity, and are sometimes ridiculed for their different characteristics (for example, they are called names such as "runt," "weakling," and "tubby").

## DEVELOPING SELF-ESTEEM

Coping with constant change and struggling with identity formation, early adolescents are insecure and vulnerable. Thus, it is difficult for them to develop a good self-concept (how a person views herself) and positive self-esteem (how a person feels about herself). For this reason, self-concept and self-esteem are at their worst during early adolescence, particularly between ages 12 and 15.

Parents increasingly recognize the importance of a good self-concept and positive self-esteem in children and are concerned that children feel good about themselves as a result. Helping early adolescents develop and maintain a good self-concept and positive self-esteem is one of the most important things parents can do for a child during these years. Children with positive self-esteem are more confident, more successful, less subject to peer pressure, better able to solve problems and cope with stress, and more likely to be happy with themselves. They have a strong sense of belonging within their families, their peer groups, and society. While many parents recognize the importance of a good self-concept and positive self-esteem, many are unclear or misguided in their understanding of how self-esteem is built.

The most popular misconception about self-esteem is that it is built when adults (parents) "make children feel good about themselves" (for example, by giving them lots of attention and doing everything possible to make them happy). The adult role in developing a child's self-esteem is what is most often misperceived or misunderstood. An adult or a parent cannot make a child feel good about himself, nor can a parent develop self-esteem *for* a child. A child has to build self-esteem *himself*. What parents and adults can do is play a major role in helping the child build his own self-esteem through guidance, direction, support, and encouragement.

Self-esteem is something that a child has to feel herself. It is a feeling that comes from within and grows within the child. It has to be built and fostered over time. Self-esteem is not something that can be imposed on a child or given to her. It is not an external thing. While external factors can support and contribute significantly to its growth, self-esteem originates and grows within the individual. Children acquire positive self-esteem when they feel competent, when they are successful, and when they are valued by others.

Much of one's self-esteem is derived from self-competence. Self-competence is developed by learning to do things successfully and independently. How can a child build competence if an adult is always doing things for him? For example, when a parent does everything to make a child happy, the child is dependent on the parent for his happiness. If a child is to become independent with time, he needs to learn to create his own happiness. Otherwise, how will he be able to function and be happy on his own in the world? How will he be able to cope in the world if his parents continually structure his environment to shelter him from failure, disappointment, and problems, thereby ensuring his happiness?

A child who can play Christmas carols on the piano for her relatives on Christmas day feels a sense of satisfaction and pride in her ability to do so. An adult has taught her to play the piano and has supported and encouraged her ability. But ultimately, it is the child who develops the capability and feels a sense of competence and pride. This pride is further reinforced by the praise and recognition she receives from relatives as they listen to her play. She is building self-esteem.

A child who learns how to sew can take pride in the clothes she produces as a result of her efforts. She learns the required skills from a teacher who provides instruction, guidance, direction, and encouragement, but ultimately the child is the one who produces the garment, choosing from a wide selection of colors, fabrics, and styles and using the skills she has been taught. The child takes pride in the fact that she made a dress to wear by herself and feels competent because she can do it again. Her sense of pride is reinforced when her parents and friends compliment her on the finished product. She is building self-esteem.

A child who has a newspaper route feels a sense of pride in that he is providing a valuable service to his customers and earning his own money at the same time. He is learning responsibility, commitment, basic principles of business, and how to earn money independently. He also receives recognition from his customers verbally and by way of tips he receives.

Adults need to help a child become competent by helping him discover his own competencies and by helping him realize that he is capable of creating his own happiness. Self-esteem grows when a child recognizes his capabilities.

Building self-esteem is a multifaceted task. It involves providing the tools a child needs to feel competent and to become successful at doing things. It includes identifying a child's strengths and helping her build on them. It requires providing recognition, encouragement, and praise for the child in his endeavors. It involves teaching a child how to solve problems when they arise and how to face and deal with disappointment and failure. A child needs to understand that it is OK to make mistakes as long as the mistakes are not intentional and as long as we learn from them.

Unconditional love and acceptance is another important component in building self-esteem. The child needs to feel that he is accepted and loved by his parents. He needs to feel that he can go to his parents at any time, even when he is in trouble, and he will not be at risk of losing their love regardless of parental objection to his behavior and regardless of parental punishment. This love is built through trust, respect, caring, consistency, and acting in the child's best interests. This love is not dependent on giving the child lots of material gifts, being permissive, and catering to the child.

Self-esteem is also built when a parent helps a child to be accepting of herself. Children need to be encouraged to do the best that they are capable of doing in any situation. They need to recognize that if they do their best, that is all that can be expected. Striving for perfection and pushing a child beyond the limits of his capabilities will hinder positive self-esteem development because the child never thinks he is good enough.

Self-esteem is something that takes time and consistent effort to build. It cannot be done overnight. It is an ongoing process, and it requires continual reinforcement through praise and encouragement. Early adolescents who have the best chance of developing positive self-esteem are those who have the love and support of their parents and friends. A child who had a good self-concept and positive self-esteem before puberty has a greater chance of keeping it intact through puberty, although there will be many ups and downs during these years.

## QUESTIONING OF VALUES

Prior to early adolescence, children see things in terms of how these things affect them. Children believe that adults are very knowledgeable about things in general, and most children believe the things their parents tell them without question. They are oblivious to things in the outside world that don't have any impact on them. At puberty, however, a child's mind begins to work like that of an adult. Children begin to be able to conceptualize, to think in an intellectual manner, and to think in more abstract terms. They can visualize and form ideas in their minds without having to see things in front of them. Based on this emerging new ability, the early adolescent begins to look at the world differently than he did as a child. As he begins to see the world from a more adult-like perspective, the early adolescent begins to form ideas on his own and relies less and less on adults for opinions, information, and judgments about things. As he observes and judges events for himself, the child suddenly discovers that the world is not the ordered universe he thought it was. For example, he was taught about right and wrong and about good and bad. But he discovers that good doesn't always prevail over evil as he previously thought it would. His previous notion of good or bad and right or wrong are quickly challenged. Most young children believe that "bad" people or people who do bad things are caught and punished; the early adolescent begins to see that this isn't always so. As a result of facing many similar situations, early adolescents become confused and don't know what to think about things. Their thinking is turned upside down, and they begin to question their values and upbringing. For example, a baseball star is caught using drugs, and a child watches this announcement on a television newscast. The early adolescent was told as a child that drugs are bad and will ruin his health and his mind. In assessing the situation for himself, the child begins to think that if the star is such a good baseball player, drugs can't be affecting him too negatively. In fact, the child concludes that the baseball star looks pretty good on television. As a result of such an event, he begins to wonder if adults know what they are talking about when they say that drugs are bad. The child begins to think that maybe drugs aren't too bad after all.

Another example is a child who is brought up in a religious home and has been taught certain traditions or ways about her religion. However, now she sees and knows other people who don't believe in God, church, or religion, and these people look normal, are nice, and seem to have happy lives. The child begins to think "I don't see God anywhere. Maybe these people are right and there is no God, so I don't need to go to church anymore."

In yet another example, parents tell their children that they should do well in school and get good grades. This is so they can go to college, get a good job, make money, and have a good life.

The child then sees a newsclip during a television show about a car salesman who couldn't read or write and became a millionaire. He begins to think maybe education isn't everything. "Look at that guy—he can't read and write and he's a millionaire," he thinks. After being exposed to a number of similar examples, the early adolescent begins to think that maybe adults don't know what they are talking about. In fact, maybe adults don't know anything. Because he has not had enough experience with life yet and is only beginning to think like an adult, he cannot see the whole picture. This is the reason for making this erroneous judgment about adults. Because he now questions the validity of what adults or his parents have told him in the past, he begins to question everything his parents or adults say in the present. As a result, early adolescents go through a period of questioning everything adults say. They also question their values and upbringing. In this way, they attempt to determine whether the values they were taught as a child are valid based on their own discoveries, experiences, and perceptions.

## KNOW-IT-ALL ATTITUDE

Having lost the simple ordered conception of the world they had in childhood, early adolescents are trying to clarify their view of the world. As they begin to discover the world from a more adult-like perspective, early adolescents suddenly see a whole range of problems previously unknown to them. As they begin to recognize problems in the adult world, early adolescents begin to analyze problems and categorize them. They see most problems in terms of black or white without acknowledging shades of gray where most problems and situations in reality exist. This thinking is shallow and oversimplified. Thus early adolescents commonly offer simple solutions to complex problems. Because the solutions are so obvious to them, early adolescents cannot understand why adults haven't thought of such answers on their own. They conclude that adults aren't smart enough. At this early stage, early adolescents do not recognize the complexities involved in problems and the shades of gray of reality. This is because of the newness of their ability to conceptualize and their total lack of experience. It can be frustrating and annoying for adults who must deal with the smug attitude exhibited by early adolescents when they think they "know it all" and have all the answers. This attitude can temporarily give early adolescents a false sense of superiority. It also predisposes them to disappointments when they find out later on that their solutions aren't so good after all.

## IDEALISM

The newfound ability to conceptualize and think more abstractly leads early adolescents to become very idealistic. That is, in contemplating their plans and situations, they tend to expect the best possible outcome in all circumstances. The best possible outcome, of course, is not always attainable. Early adolescents making elaborate idealistic plans soon discover this fact. When their idealistic plans don't materialize as expected, early adolescents become very upset. Their idealism therefore predisposes them to disappointments, disillusionment, and cynicism.

In their search for truth and wisdom in the ways of the world, and in their first encounters with thinking about life, early adolescents are very altruistic. They want to right all the wrongs in the world, and they want to find ways to make the world a happy place. They enjoy having philosophical discussions about humanistic issues, environmental issues, and the like. They are very much against any kind of oppression and will usually side with the underdog in any situation.

Early adolescents can also be very enthusiastic about things. When they develop an interest in something, they will work hard to make it work out. The enthusiasm, however, is not always about doing things adults feel is appropriate or worthwhile.

# CRITICISM

As early adolescents begin to view the world more as adults, they begin to see that there are many things wrong with the world, its people, and everyday life in general. They become critical of many things, especially if things aren't "the way they are supposed to be." Being able to analyze and identify faults and weaknesses, they also become critical of people. Seeing what's wrong with people or things and being able to verbalize it confirms for them that they are successful in their new ability to think more analytically or like an adult. It also makes them think they are clever.

However, although early adolescents are critical of others, especially their parents—complaining about the way people dress, how they look and the way "things should be"—they do not like to be criticized by anyone themselves and are easily offended by criticism. Because early adolescents are very insecure and lack self-confidence during puberty, they become easily frustrated and upset with criticism, especially when it is directed at them from adult sources. In their discovery of themselves and the world, and in trying to adjust to the many changes they are experiencing, it is difficult for early adolescents to feel confident and secure about anything. When they try hard to speak, dress, or behave in what they feel is an appropriate manner and then are criticized for doing so, it makes them feel even more insecure and less confident. They also become frustrated and say things like "It's no use. No matter what I do, it's never right." Thus, although they think it is all right for them to criticize others, criticism from adults and other sources is not easily tolerated, even when it concerns things they are prone to criticize themselves.

# SEXUAL FEELINGS AND AFFECTION

During puberty, early adolescents develop many new feelings based on the sexual awakening and the development they are experiencing. Feelings of affection become more intense, especially toward members of the opposite sex. They also begin to have sexual feelings, which are often combined with feelings of affection. This results in them feeling that they are in love. Feelings of love and sexuality can make early adolescents very uncomfortable and confused. Since most of them are experiencing the feelings for the first time, they don't know how to act or react. Thus, it can be a frightening experience for them because they don't understand what is going on or what will happen next as a result of the feelings they have.

Early adolescents, especially girls, may experience a tingling sensation in their stomachs as well as an intense, exciting, fireworks kind of feeling toward a member of the opposite sex. Thinking about the object of their affection all the time, they feel they are in love. While adults consider these feelings "puppy love" or infatuation, to the early adolescent they are very real. They insist that they are in love. Adults "just don't understand." Individually, early adolescents feel that they are the only ones who have ever experienced these emotions. For adults to suggest otherwise means, once again, they just don't understand. Their feelings can also be unreciprocated in that the object of their affection is unaware of the love they feel (for example, infatuation with movie or music stars).

Boys are more likely to have strong sexual feelings at this age as opposed to the infatuation felt by girls. As the sex drive develops, sexual tension builds up. Most early adolescent boys will experiment and find pleasurable feelings and ways to release sexual tension through self-stimulation. Masturbation usually provides boys with their first sexual experience (ejaculation). As their sex drives develop, boys become very uncomfortable with their new sexual feelings as they struggle with nocturnal emissions (wet dreams) and involuntary erections. They don't know what to do or think about these things. They don't know why they are having these feelings, and they are frightened because they don't know what will happen next. Boys have their first such experiences around the age of 13. Early adolescents engage in masturbation as a way of discovering their own bodies and feelings as well as to release sexual tensions.

During puberty, early adolescents become more sensitive to outward expressions of physical affection from their parents, siblings, or other relatives. Although kissing their grandparents good-bye or their parents good-night may be OK for some early adolescents if done in private, almost all early adolescents detest any demonstration of affection from adults in public, especially in front of their peers. They fear ridicule, social disapproval, or rejection by their friends who relate this type of behavior to babies and children.

## THE EARLY ADOLESCENT VIEW
## OF SEXUALITY

The early adolescent view of sex and sexuality is seldom rooted in truth or reality. Rather, it is distorted and unrealistic, and filled with misinformation and myths. Early adolescents are constantly bombarded with sexual behaviors, language, innuendo, and stimuli in the media. Sex is pervasive in television programming, advertising, music, videos, and many other areas of society. Because what they see in the media appears real, early adolescents are strongly affected by it. In the media, sex is almost always portrayed as the ultimate act of pleasure and self-fulfillment—as the most desired of all things. As they become young adults and sexually mature, early adolescents look to adults as models for their behavior. As a result of being exposed to so much sexual behavior in the media on a continual basis, many early adolescents form the impression that sex is of ultimate importance in the adult world because it appears that everything revolves around it.

In the media, sexual activity usually takes place in romantic or otherwise perfect settings where attractive adults passionately fall into each other's arms and proceed with sexual activity without any consideration of responsibility, pregnancy, birth control, or transmission of AIDS or venereal disease. Characters frequently have passionate encounters with multiple partners. The fact that the people engaging in these encounters hardly know each other is also not considered. Because of the fantasy attached to sexual behavior in the media, it is important that the early adolescent learn to distinguish fact from fiction with regard to sexual behavior. An alarming number of early adolescents erroneously believe the following:

- If they go out on a date, sex is expected.
- Because they are sexually mature, they should become sexually active.
- Because they are becoming young adults, they should become active sexually; having sex is the "adult" thing to do, and it appears to them that "everyone" is doing it.
- They will be labeled as "prudes" if they don't become sexually active at a young age.
- They need to dress in a "sexy" manner and need to act sexual in order to be appealing to members of the opposite sex.
- Sex and affection are one and the same.

## EMOTIONAL MATURITY

Emotional maturity (that is, the ability to control emotions that are socially disapproved of and to relieve emotions in a socially acceptable way) in early adolescents takes time. It is also dependent in part on the degree of intellectual development a child has achieved. Emotional maturity typically increases at ages 13 to 14 in both sexes with girls leading boys in this area. Early adolescents continue to refine their emotions throughout the teen years.

# 4

# Coping with Early Adolescent Emotions

Learning to live with the unpredictable nature of early adolescent emotions is not always easy. It is difficult to accept that a child who was once relatively agreeable and easy to manage can be so moody, irritable, argumentative, unpredictable, and impulsive. However, since little can be done to stop the inevitable process of early adolescent development and the emotional instability associated with it, parents and others who work with early adolescents can only prepare themselves as best they can to deal with it. Knowing the type of emotional behavior to expect and recognizing why it occurs can help one feel more confident and secure in dealing with early adolescents.

## DEALING WITH
## NEGATIVE EMOTIONS OBJECTIVELY

An important thing parents can do during early adolescence is to learn that they should not take personally the many criticisms, negative remarks, and emotions that early adolescents frequently direct toward them. A parent becomes an easy target for early adolescent anger and frustration. Being with the child for extended periods of time, a parent cannot escape the brunt of these emotional outbursts. Rather than feel hurt or under attack, parents need to try to remove themselves emotionally from the remarks and deal with the situation as objectively as possible. Although this is easier said than done, it can be extremely helpful. For example, let's consider Jane's outburst (see Chapter 3) in which she criticized her mother for "making spaghetti again." Her mother's initial tendency might be to feel hurt that her meal isn't good and that she is making her daughter unhappy as a result. Her mother should stop herself from feeling hurt immediately after the comment is made. Then she should allow herself to examine the situation objectively to determine why the comment was made. She might ask herself, "Am I making spaghetti too often?" As she thinks about it, she realizes that she hasn't made spaghetti for quite a long while. Thus, she can immediately tell herself that her daughter's outburst was not really meant for her. It appears, rather, that her daughter is frustrated or angry with something or someone else and is taking out her frustrations and anger on her. Thus the mother need not feel hurt or upset or take the comments personally. Although it is not always possible to look at these outbursts objectively, it can help parents feel less hurt. It can also help them to sort out those situations or events that are genuine and deserving of attention or resolution and those that are not.

## ACCEPTING WHAT IS NORMAL

The next thing that parents can do to prepare themselves for early adolescent emotional development is to learn to accept what is considered normal behavior for this age group. Be prepared for the everyday moods, hates, loves, and annoyances of these children. Expect that early adolescents will be self-centered, angry, critical, and impulsive. Accept that they will exaggerate, experiment with things, have changing interests, and adopt a "know-it-all" attitude. Expect that early adolescents will be self-conscious and insecure and that they will worry about what they look like and what others think of them. While you may not like any of this behavior typical of early adolescents, learning to accept it as normal will help you to feel less frustrated and stressed about it. Recognizing that you are probably not the cause of this behavior is important.

## REMEMBERING YOUR OWN EARLY ADOLESCENCE

While coping with early adolescents is likely to be difficult for parents, it is just as difficult or more so for the child. Remember that you were once an early adolescent child yourself, and your parents probably had some difficulty trying to cope with your behavior in much the same way that you are having difficulty coping with your child's behavior. When trying to understand early adolescent emotions and behavior, it is helpful to think back to a time when you were the same age. Think about how you felt during those years. What was your perception of adult life then? Were you moody and unpredictable? Did you argue with your parents? Did you hurt their feelings and say things you didn't mean or shouldn't have said? Were you worried about how you looked and what people thought of you? These are some questions to consider in reviewing your own early adolescent years. You will probably agree in retrospect that they were not easy years for you or your parents.

## KEEPING BEHAVIOR UNDER CONTROL

While sympathy toward the early adolescent child and an understanding of her difficulties are needed, it does not mean that all of the child's negative behavior should be accepted or that it should be allowed to get out of control. The child should not be permitted to make everyone in the family miserable as a result of her behavior. Sympathy and understanding must be tempered with parental authority and control. When early adolescents engage in behavior that is not acceptable, they should be told that it is not acceptable. They also need to be told why. While many of the negative behaviors of early adolescents will be repeats of simple misbehavior of the past, many of the behaviors they engage in will be new to them and part of the experimentation process. Thus they will be doing many things for the first time. They may also do things to see what they can get away with. And at times, they may do things out of ignorance or indifference; they simply don't know any better. It is important to explain to early adolescents the reasons why their behavior is not acceptable. They are becoming young adults and need to recognize the adult way of doing things. They also need to know how their actions affect others. With an intellectual understanding of their behavior, it is hoped they will modify or correct it in the future.

The explanation you give to early adolescents concerning unacceptable behavior can be brief (for example, "You're late"), or it can involve more extensive discussion. The goal is to give your reasoning for not accepting the behavior. While the child may be given an opportunity to break into the discussion at some point (that is, to present her arguments or give her reason or excuse), it should not turn into a long-winded debate in which you as a parent end up explaining or arguing about every little detail. You are the parent, and she is the child; that relationship should remain. While you may consider your child's input or point of view, as a parent, you do not have to justify everything you say or do. However, if you give no explanation and no reasoning and impose strict authority on the child, she will eventually become resentful of you. She may feel that you are treating her as a little child, or she may not be sure of what she is doing wrong or why she is being punished. Rebellion toward you may escalate as a result. Another difficulty that can develop if this is carried out over an extended period is that the child will become alienated. Once this happens, the child becomes so resentful of you that she doesn't care what she does anymore, as long as it is not what you want her to do.

Let us review a few examples of misbehavior we have previously discussed (see Chapter 3) from the perspective of how they might be dealt with. The example of John's father calling him downstairs to see his Uncle Bill, and John refusing because he was listening to music, might be dealt with as follows. After the uncle leaves, later in the day, John's father might say to him, "John, I was embarrassed with your behavior toward Uncle Bill today. He wanted to see you and talk with you, and you wouldn't come downstairs because you were listening to music. Think of how he must have felt. You probably hurt his feelings. He was very anxious to see you, and you gave him the impression that listening to your music was more important to you than he was. I was very embarrassed to hear your comments shouted downstairs while Uncle Bill was listening. Next time this happens, I would like you to . . . (give further directions here). Examples might include (1) say you'll be down in a minute or two rather than say things to hurt other people's feelings and (2) come down when you are called.

Once the guests had gone home at Cheryl's house, her mother could have discussed some etiquette with her pertaining to house guests. She might say, "Cheryl, when we have guests over, I would like you to spend a minute or two with them when they arrive. You can say hello and ask them how they are and talk with them for a few minutes. Then, if you want to, you can go to your room for the rest of the time. It is not polite to ignore guests, especially when they are happy to see you." Cheryl might object, "But Mom, they are going to say things like 'How you've grown' and stuff like that, and it makes me feel like a baby." Cheryl's mother might counter, "But that's how older people are. They don't mean anything by it, and it makes them happy. Since it won't hurt you to hear it, try to be pleasant with them."

Jane's angry outburst about why her mother made spaghetti again should have been stopped once her mother realized that Jane's anger was misplaced. She might say, "Jane, I have not made spaghetti for several weeks. I can see that you are angry about something. When you settle down and are ready to talk in a calmer tone, we'll do that." Jane may choose not to tell her mother about the source of her anger, or she may deny that her anger is about something else. However, if Jane does reveal the source of her anger, it will give her an opportunity to talk about it and vent her frustration about her friend, thus allowing her to "get it out of her system" without further attacking anyone innocent.

In talking about things with early adolescents, they may say that all you do is criticize them. When this happens, you can indicate to them that you are trying to tell and show them how adults act in these situations. Since they will soon be young adults themselves, they will be expected to act in a more adult-like manner. However, do not expect children to appreciate your advice or to be openly accepting of your reprimands. They will not like being reprimanded or criticized any more during early adolescence than during any other time. However, whether or not it appears to be the case, they will be internalizing what you say.

## HELPING EARLY ADOLESCENTS WITH PROBLEMS

Early adolescents are very anxiety-prone, worrying about things that appear insignificant to adults. When a child approaches a parent with a problem or question, it is important to listen. Do not dismiss the problem as unimportant. If the problem were unimportant, the child would not be asking for advice. A problem may appear inconsequential in the judgment of a parent who is much older, wiser, and experienced in the ways of the world. To the child, however, it may be monumental. Adults should try to see the problem from the child's perspective. For example, Robin does not want to go to a social event because she has a big pimple in the middle of her cheek, and she is afraid everyone will notice it and will stare or laugh at her. She is in tears because she got a new dress and shoes to wear for this event. And now, she has this ugly pimple, which ruins everything. A mother might approach the problem by telling the child that it is normal for teens to have pimples, that other teens there will have pimples too, that her pimple isn't that bad, and that other people aren't going to notice it as much as she thinks. In an attempt to help her with her problem, the mother might then find some makeup that can be applied directly to the pimple to diminish its appearance.

While you might point out to a child that she is exaggerating a problem, it is not useful to dismiss it. Telling children things like, "Oh, that's nothing" or "Don't worry about it," does not help the child significantly. Children interpret these statements as a lack of understanding or interest. In the above example, Robin felt better and more confident after her mother helped her deal with her problem. If her mother had said that it was nothing to worry about and then left it at that, Robin would have remained upset and less confident, and might have convinced herself not to attend the event.

Also, if a child presents a problem or question and is immediately given a lecture or is spoken to in an accusatory manner, the child will be hesitant to discuss things in the future. For example, Suzanne asks her mother what she should do if a boy tries to kiss her. If Suzanne's mother immediately responds by saying things like, "Who is trying to kiss you? Is it that new boy down the street you've been walking to school with? I knew he was no good," then Suzanne may not want to approach her mother for advice in the future. Suzanne's mother is more likely to gain Suzanne's trust by answering the question more directly by saying, "Well, Suzanne, it depends on many things, like how old you are or whether you like the boy or not." While the problem may be a real one for Suzanne, as a boy may have tried to kiss her, often early adolescents are just curious about things and are only asking for information or clarification about how to deal with a potential situation. The child may also be asking about a problem for a friend who is afraid to ask her own mother. So the way in which a question or problem is dealt with will have an impact in the future on whether the child will seek your advice, or the advice of her peers. Even though you may be "dying to know" if the question or problem is related to the child (that is, did a boy really try to kiss her), try to restrain yourself for a while to avoid making your curiosity the focus of the discussion. Later on, after you have dealt with the child's question or problem, you can ask about your curiosities.

## LISTENING

In dealing with early adolescent problems in general, the most important thing you can do is listen. Many times early adolescents don't really want advice. They just want someone who cares to listen to them. At this point and in these circumstances, offering advice may make an early adolescent more frustrated. Many early adolescent problems stem from children's lack of experience with life and their perspective of things in puberty. Although they may indeed want advice, at times they just want reassurance about something or consolation and encouragement when things aren't going right. Other times, talking to you is a way to relieve frustration or anxiety about something. Try to determine which of these is the case and deal with it accordingly. Also, remember that because early adolescents are so changeable, what appears to be a problem one day may not be a problem the next. That does not minimize the problem. When a child approaches you with a problem, it must be dealt with because the child considers it significant at that point in time.

It may also be useful, when appropriate, to relate similar or relevant experiences you had as an early adolescent, as well as how you felt and how the problem was solved. For example, a father might say to his son, "When I was your age, I was smaller in size than the average boys in my class, and this big kid, Mark, was always picking on me and calling me names. So one day I decided that I had had enough and . . . ."

## PARENTS AS IMPORTANT SOURCES OF VALUES

During puberty, early adolescents begin to question the values and beliefs they were taught as children. Their statements and questions about whether such long-held values and beliefs are valid often shock their parents. However, this is a normal activity for these children. Early adolescents must discover or rediscover their values and beliefs for themselves through trial and error, experimentation, and experience. Being told what to believe and value by adults isn't good enough for them anymore.

Having said that, it is important to recognize that parents are significant reference sources in the development of a child's attitudes, values, and beliefs about life in general. If these concepts were developed and applied during childhood and remained on a solid foundation during the childhood years, early adolescents will most likely end up with them as adults. In the long run, solid values instilled by parents win out even though the child may wander off course during the teen years. Early adolescents who battle their parents' beliefs and values during puberty will often adopt these values themselves as adults. Parents should therefore adhere to their values in the face of the child's questioning, even if it appears that the child is not listening, doesn't care, or isn't interested.

## TALKING THINGS OUT

The importance of talking to early adolescents about their behavior and beliefs has been mentioned several times thus far. It needs to be said, however, that early adolescents do not necessarily like listening to your comments, remarks, "lectures," and discussions. They do not like parents telling them what to do, telling them what is right, and so on. Parents often feel that they are wasting their time talking to their children when the children react negatively or indifferently to their discussions and remarks. However, be assured that parental discussions and lectures, if not carried to an extreme, are effective in the long run. Early adolescents' minds are receptive, and they will internalize what has been said, even though it doesn't appear to be that way. When children find themselves in a tough situation in which they must make a decision, they remember what their parents said about things.

They have something to fall back on. It is important, therefore, that parents not assume that their talks and lectures go unheeded. Although that may appear to be the case in the short run, in the long run, as early adolescents acquire more experience with life, most of them realize that their parents were right and were looking out for their best interests.

## POSITIVE BEHAVIOR

Most of our discussion thus far has dealt with many of the negative behaviors of the early adolescent child. One thing we must not forget is that we must also deal with the positive behavior. Early adolescents need to be praised when they behave appropriately and when they do good things. Tell them when you are proud of them. Tell them when they look good or make an interesting intellectual observation. In our discussion, we have dwelt mainly on the negative aspects of early adolescent behavior because the negative aspects are more difficult to deal with. But early adolescents need plenty of positive reinforcement on which they can build self-confidence. It will help them feel good about themselves and more secure about things in general. It also provides them with encouragement to maintain good behavior in the future. Use positive reinforcement and praise early adolescents as often as circumstances warrant.

## HESITANCY TO EXPRESS AFFECTION

Early adolescents are hesitant to express love or emotions toward parents. Many parents interpret this to mean that they are no longer loved, appreciated, or needed, but this is not so. Early adolescents associate affectionate behavior toward parents with babies and childhood, and they do not want to associate themselves in any way with babies and childhood. Thus, while some early adolescents will be affectionate with parents in private, most feel "stupid" expressing affection toward parents (or other older relatives for that matter), and may no longer do so during the early adolescent years. However, despite the fact that most early adolescents no longer feel comfortable with physical expressions of affection, they do need to feel loved and be continually reassured that they are loved.

## NEED FOR SECURITY AND STABILITY

Throughout their emotional evolution, early adolescents remain insecure. Everything in their lives is changing: their bodies, emotions, identity, intellect, and so on. They need to have some things in their lives that are stable. Unfortunately, there aren't many possible choices. Home and family life are among the few possibilities. As a result, it is important to provide a stable and secure home and environment for children during the early adolescent years. Even though expressing affection no longer appeals to them, early adolescents need a secure and stable relationship with their parents and want to be sure of their parents' love for them. They need constant reassurance of their worth and abilities and also need continual support from adult sources in the face of constant change. This is in spite of the fact that they so often appear unappreciative and indifferent toward their parents.

# 5

# Social Development

As they become more adult-like in physical appearance, early adolescents want to be more adult-like in their behavior, particularly in the social contexts of their lives. To accomplish this, early adolescents must achieve independence from adults and establish an identity of their own. This is a difficult transitional process that takes several years to complete.

## DEVELOPING AN IDENTITY

One of the most important tasks a child must accomplish during early adolescence is the achievement of an identity. Before puberty, a child's identity is tied to that of her parents and family. During early adolescence, children begin to look inward to see who they are. They begin to view themselves as entities separate from their parents and families. Who am I? How did I get this way? How am I coming across to others? These are some of the questions early adolescents need to answer for themselves during these in-between years. During this process, the early adolescent's perception of himself (that is, self-concept) undergoes tremendous reorientation as he begins to assess himself from an entirely new perspective. During the process of discovering who they are and their role in the world around them, early adolescents are in constant inward turmoil, experiencing much confusion, many paradoxes, and many emotional ups and downs. It is a frustrating time for them.

## ACHIEVING INDEPENDENCE

Another important task a child must accomplish during early adolescence is the attainment of a degree of independence as a person. This contrasts with years of dependence on parents, family, teachers, and other adults for guidance and direction. Before puberty, children rely on their families for almost everything they need, physically and emotionally. During puberty, they seek to achieve independence from adults.

Early adolescents are able to work toward these goals as a result of changes in their thinking ability. During puberty, children begin to think in a more adult-like manner. They begin to conceptualize and to analyze situations. They begin to think in a more intellectual manner, to manipulate ideas, to hypothesize, and to seek possibilities. With this new ability, early adolescents set out to discover who they are, their role in society, what the world is like, and what life is all about. This is not an easy task.

## PERCEPTION OF ADULT LIFE

As children become aware of their changing bodies, they know they will soon be adults. As they study the world from a new perspective, they focus a great deal on the lives of adults and the adult world around them. Looking at adults' lives with a still somewhat child-like perspective, early adolescents' initial perception of adults is that their lives are wonderful. They conclude that this is so because adults can do whatever they want to do. They are free from parental authority, they don't have to follow parental rules, they don't have to be home by a certain time, they can buy whatever they want, they can go anywhere they please, and so on. As a result of these perceptions, early adolescents are very excited about the prospect of becoming adults and being free to do as they please. What early adolescents don't see at this time are the responsibilities and restrictions associated with adult lives, like getting a job, having to get up for work every morning, supporting oneself, supporting a family, and making difficult decisions.

The media perpetuates the early adolescent perception of adult lives in the way adults are portrayed on television; in movies, videos, and advertisements; and on billboards and posters. Because of their new ability to perceive things from a more adult-like perspective and because they have not yet formed their own values and beliefs about life, early adolescents are very impressionable and vulnerable. Thus, they are easily influenced by the fantasies of adult lives portrayed in the media. Vulnerability peaks during early adolescence.

Adults have to contend with the same media fantasies about life that early adolescents do, but because they are older, wiser, and more experienced, adults can judge for themselves what is realistic and what is not. They know that what they see on television and in the movies is often exaggerated or distorted and seldom resembles reality. For adults, the media provides fantasy as a means of escaping the realities, responsibilities, and problems that exist in everyday life. For early adolescents who are not yet mature enough in their thinking or experienced with life, the fantasy is reality. For this period of time in their lives, early adolescents develop somewhat unrealistic ideas and expectations about adult life. Some examples include the following:

- Attractive men and women are always popular and happy.
- People who drink always have fun and a good time.
- When men or boys drink, they attract good-looking girls.
- Girls who wear sexy or revealing clothing will be popular with men and will have plenty of boyfriends and dates.
- Sex is no big deal. It is expected on dates.

- Wearing certain brands of clothing or using certain brands of products will significantly improve one's looks.
- Attractiveness guarantees love from the opposite sex.
- Smoking is sexy and cool.

Soap operas and other related romantic types of programs and movies also perpetuate many unrealistic perceptions about adult life and relationships. For example, a girl becomes pregnant on a soap opera, and suddenly several doctors and lawyers are fighting over who the father is and who will get to marry the girl. This rarely, if ever, happens. But because it is a theme repeated so often in movies and on television, early adolescents may not see the situation realistically. Of course, as early adolescents get older, they discover that life is not what they thought it was, and they are disappointed and disillusioned as the reality begins to set in.

## EMULATION OF ADULT BEHAVIOR

Early adolescents idealize adults. As a result, they want to be like adults and want to do adult things (for example, wear makeup, smoke, swear, drink, and have sex). In the process, early adolescents try to disassociate themselves with childhood and anything that is related or reminiscent of childhood. By emulating adult behavior, early adolescents feel more adult-like. However, they lack not only the experience and vision to see the responsibilities that go with adult behavior, but also the consequences that can result from adult behavior. These consequences, including pregnancy, venereal disease, and accidents related to alcohol use, are seldom portrayed in the media.

## INVINCIBILITY

Because early adolescents are so idealistic in their thinking, even when they are told the consequences of the adult behavior, they feel they are invincible, believing that nothing bad will happen to them. They cannot project the consequences of their behaviors into the future. There is plenty of evidence to confirm this. For example, many young teen girls pressured into having sex to "prove" their love or for social acceptance thought they would not become pregnant. Statistics show, however, that one out of four teen girls do get pregnant the first time they have sex.

An even simpler example is when early adolescents refuse to wear hats, scarfs, gloves, and other appropriate clothing in cold weather because they feel that they won't get cold, despite the fact that temperatures are below freezing and other people are bundled up for the cold.

## FLUCTUATIONS IN BEHAVIOR

While early adolescents have a strong desire to increase their independence and personal decision making during puberty, they are, at the same time, reluctant to leave the security of childhood where they feel physically and emotionally safe, and where they are protected from the pressures of the outside world.

As a result of being caught between their desire to be safe and secure and their desire for freedom and independence, early adolescent behavior fluctuates from mature to childish. They act like children one moment and like adults the next. Early adolescents vacillate between their desire to be regulated and given direction by adults and their demand for independence. One instant they want adult input; the next they don't. Parents are caught in between, not knowing what to do. Offering a child advice on one occasion may be accepted, whereas in another similar circumstance, the advice instigates a tirade of emotion toward the parent, who is accused of being interfering, nagging, and so on. When early adolescents do seek adult input or opinion, they reserve the right to accept or reject it if the suggestions are not suitable or acceptable to them.

While early adolescents become increasingly able to accept

responsibility, they want the security of not having to accept the consequences of their actions or mistakes. So from an adult perspective, it appears that early adolescents want the best of both worlds: the security of childhood, the freedom of adulthood, and the ability to pick and choose from each depending on their needs.

## EXPERIMENTATION

Through the process of discovering who they are, early adolescents engage in much experimentation. Experimentation is a normal process through which early adolescents attempt to determine what is right for them, what they like, what they are good at, and so on. They may experiment with relatively harmless things such as hairstyle, makeup, and even style of writing, to those of a more negative nature such as smoking, drinking, drugs, and sex. During the process of identity formation, the early adolescent constantly tests out new identities, seeking confirmation of the characteristics of his or her new self. The early adolescent needs to test out various social roles and identities in order to develop one that will be his or her own.

## PREOCCUPATION WITH THE SELF

As early adolescents discover who they are and begin to establish an identity, they go through an intense period of preoccupation with themselves. Being egocentric, they become focused on themselves and their needs, often to the exclusion of others. As a result, they become increasingly inconsiderate of others in the family or engage in what appears to be very selfish behavior. For example, early adolescents may stay on the telephone for long periods of time, even though they know that others may be expecting a call or may want to make a call. This is especially annoying to parents because early adolescents often talk on the phone for an inordinate amount of time for what appears to be no important reason, just idle chatter. Yet when asked to get off the phone, they continually resist.

The early adolescent girl often stays in the bathroom fussing with her hair and appearance for long periods of time before school in the morning, even though she knows her siblings and others need to use the bathroom to get ready for school or work themselves. Parents frustrated with this behavior often make comments like, "You would think she was the only person living here." However, the early adolescent sees what she is doing as necessary. Because she fails to differentiate between her own preoccupation with herself and what others are thinking and concerned with, she assumes that other people are as preoccupied with her and her appearance as she is herself. Thus, she rationalizes that the extra time and care she takes to get herself ready is warranted. Because they feel they are constantly being observed or talked about by others, early adolescents prepare for school or a social event as if they were preparing for this "imaginary" audience.

## DISREGARD FOR INCONVENIENCING OTHERS

Focused on their own needs and wants, at times, early adolescents develop a complete disregard for inconveniencing parents and other adults to get what they need or want. For example, Karen wants her mother to drive her to her friend's house just as her mother begins to prepare for guests who will be arriving shortly. Peter wants help with his homework at nine o'clock Sunday night when a documentary his father has been looking forward to watching comes on television. When his father asks Peter why he didn't do his homework earlier in the day or weekend, Peter gives an excuse and then adds, "Well if you won't help me, I won't do it," making his father feel guilty and shifting the responsibility for the negative consequences of his actions to his father. Even more annoying to adults than being inconvenienced by early adolescents is that when adults go out of their way to do things for them, it often appears to be taken for granted or is not appreciated.

## THE VIEW THAT PARENTS
## DON'T KNOW ANYTHING

Early adolescents frequently feel that their parents are out of step with society and societal norms. Watching families and other teens on television or in the movies leads them to believe that what they see in the media is reality in society today. If they perceive that their own family lifestyle does not match their vision of the media norm, they label their parents as old-fashioned and different. At the same time, they think that everyone else's family and parents are in step with what is going on in society. This, of course, is because they are not actually there to see how these other families live. As a result of this misguided thinking, early adolescents conclude that their parents "don't know anything," while other adults know best. This can be extremely frustrating for parents who worry that their efforts to look out for the best interests of the child are fruitless.

Early adolescents can make statements like, "I don't want to eat meat anymore. Kelsey's mother says it is bad for you, and she should know. She's a nurse." Or, "I'm not going to church with you on Sunday. Gary's uncle says you don't need to go to church on Sunday. You can pray just as well at home."

Young adolescents sometimes manipulate their parents into allowing them to do certain things by telling them that they are old-fashioned and different from other parents. Children will use phrases like, "Michael's parents let him do it" or "Everyone else will be there." They do this to get their own way. "Everyone else" may mean one or two others. Parents, however, face somewhat of a dilemma. Their instincts and values tell them not to allow the child his own way, but at the same time, they don't want to deny their child things that are considered normal for the age group. The fact is that most parents are in a similar situation, struggling with their child and trying to decide what to do under the circumstances.

## REJECTION OF THE FAMILY

During early adolescence, it is normal for children to disassociate themselves from their families. Finding their own identity means rejecting the family from which they once derived their identity. To achieve a sense of self, early adolescents must psychologically separate themselves from their parents and the family unit. Thus, during early adolescence, family norms and values are frequently devalued. There is often indifference toward younger or older brothers and sisters and extended members of the family (grandparents, aunts, uncles, and so on). Early adolescents don't like to be seen in public with their families and feel embarrassed to be seen with their parents by their peers.

During puberty, early adolescents begin to resist participating in many family-oriented activities. They may not want to involve themselves in activities with their parents or siblings, preferring to do things with their friends and peers. Early adolescents begin to resist going on family vacations that they formerly enjoyed (such as going to a cottage, to the beach, camping), unless they can bring a friend. They want to go to the beach, theme parks, and so on, but with their friends, not their families.

## ROLE MODELS AND IDOLS

Early adolescents have a strong need to have an idol, an ideal adult role model. Parents cannot fulfill this role because early adolescents, with their new ability to analyze and intellectualize, are becoming aware of their parents' faults and weaknesses. As a result, they may reject having their parents as role models because they now consider their parents flawed. Thus, young adolescents tend to seek out adults who are sufficiently removed from their immediate environment and whose faults are not readily evident. Early adolescents believe these other adults do not have faults, because they themselves are not with these individuals long enough to see what their faults are. It is therefore difficult to convince them otherwise. While sometimes the role model chosen by the child will be a relative, neighbor, or friend's parent, he or she can also be an adult with less desirable traits or of questionable character.

Other related practices of early adolescents include having "crushes" on idealized adults or engaging in a form of hero worship of teen idols, rock music stars, movie stars, and so on. These types of attachments are relatively short-lived.

## SOCIALIZING

Early adolescents are limited as to where they can go outside of their homes to socialize. They are not yet old enough to drive and have little money to spend as compared with older teens with part-time jobs. In larger cities they are limited to going places along bus routes, while in small towns they are limited to places within walking distance of their homes. On this basis, early adolescents find places where they can get together with their friends and socialize away from their families. They are often seen "hanging around" with friends at a corner store. They particularly like frequenting malls, where they can meet their friends, socialize, and window shop. While at a mall, they can also engage in more negative behavior such as poking fun or laughing at adults and other kids who walk by. Many adults are repulsed by such young groups of "disrespectful" kids marauding around malls, especially if they are smoking, swearing, wearing weird clothes and makeup, and laughing at other people.

## TALKING

One of early adolescents' favorite social activities is talking. Talking doesn't cost them money, and it doesn't require transportation if done over the phone. Early adolescent girls in particular, can talk for hours about nothing. Spurts of giggling are common in early adolescent conversation, especially when they talk about "grown-up" things, such as body changes and boys. Girls' conversations frequently focus on boys, pop music, their idols, and romance.

## REBELLION AND INDEPENDENCE

For them to feel that they are becoming adults, early adolescents want to do more things on their own, make their own decisions, and be free of parental authority and control. To do this, they need to disassociate themselves from adult influence, thereby convincing themselves that they don't need adults in their lives. The way in which early adolescents express their independence from adults is to rebel against them. This rebellion and defiance of adult wishes, control, and authority convinces early adolescents that they are becoming adult-like. Therefore, the function of early adolescent rebelliousness is not to make adults miserable, but to reinforce the process of becoming free from dependence or adult authority. While is it very difficult for adults to endure the rebellion, it is an essential psychological process that early adolescents must experience in order to successfully achieve a state of independence and an identity separate from adults.

During the process of rebellion, early adolescents often do the opposite of what adults want them to do. Over time, this becomes increasingly annoying and intolerable to those who have to cope with them. Parents want children home and safe by a certain time. Early adolescents want to stay out late and socialize at the malls. Parents don't want children to smoke because of the health hazards and the addictive factor. Early adolescents want to be like adults, and smoking makes them feel grown up. Parents want children to do well academically in school so that they can go to college or get a good job when they finish school. Early adolescents go to school to socialize, make friends, and show off their latest clothes, hairstyles, and acquisitions. The list goes on and on. In early adolescence, the greatest amount of turmoil and aggressive behavior toward parents usually occurs between ages 12 and 14. Argumentativeness is also most pronounced during the 12- to 14-year period, with girls being worse than boys.

In being rebellious, early adolescents are also testing the confines of the adult value system. Adult standards and conventions are often ignored, ridiculed, and defied in a child's quest for independence. Making fun of anything adults do, what they wear, how they speak, and their mannerisms and ideas is common.

## THE IMPORTANCE OF FRIENDS

Reaching early adolescence and having rejected adults and their values, early adolescents have nowhere to turn but to their peers for guidance, support, and advice. During the 10- to 14-year age period, friends take on increasing significance. In fact, friendships and peer interaction become more important than anything else in their lives. This is in contrast to the 8- to 10-year age period when children do not have the same need for social interaction.

Initially, peer groups and friendships are formed with children of the same sex. Early adolescents find security in the companionship of others their own age who have the same interests and values and whose backgrounds are similar. At the age of 12 to 13, early adolescents develop an interest in forming friendships with persons of the opposite sex.

Having friends during early adolescence is important. In fact, it is so important that the number of friends a person has becomes a direct measure of his or her popularity. Since early adolescents continually look to their peers for the acceptance and support they need, their desire for social acceptance leads to gregariousness. Early adolescents often adopt a personality they feel will attract friends rather than being and acting like themselves. Thus, their personalities can change from one instance to another, becoming very chameleon-like.

## THE PEER GROUP AND PEER PRESSURE

Becoming a member of a group is also important to early adolescents. Gaining the acceptance of a peer group (a group of similar-aged children who socialize together) is vital. Again, to gain acceptance, early adolescents will often behave in a manner that will allow them to be accepted by their chosen peer group. Once accepted, early adolescents must be loyal to the standards of dress, speech, and behavior typical of the group. To retain the group's acceptance and approval as well as to avoid rejection, early adolescents often say or do things they wouldn't ordinarily say or do. Peer pressure (pressure to behave and speak in a certain way or to conform to the standards, norms, and behavior of a certain group) is rooted in early adolescent feelings of insecurity, self-consciousness, and low self-esteem. These traits can be traced back to physical and emotional development. Not having friends or a peer group during puberty can be devastating to a child.

Because having friends and pleasing friends is so important, the friendships formed and the people with whom they are formed are extremely important. Friends can have a direct and significant influence in determining a child's future direction in life. Getting in with the wrong crowd during early adolescence can have devastating long-term effects. If a child chooses to become part of a group whose behavior is deviant, he will have to act like other members of the group and do what they do, in order to be accepted. If members of the group become involved in crime, the child will be pressured to do so if he wants to remain part of the group.

By the same token, getting in with the right crowd during

early adolescence can have a positive effect on a child. Others in the group will generate pressure to do well academically, to be involved in family and school life, to do well in sports and related activities, and to steer away from misconduct.

Both types of peer groups have a code of conduct, and early adolescents in both groups will be subjected to peer pressure as well as many of the characteristics of experimentation and conformity. The difference is that the pressure to experiment and conform in the positive peer group will be centered on doing things (such as swearing, wearing makeup, or wearing weird clothes) that will not ultimately endanger the child's safety or cause the child any long-term harm. Early adolescents in these positive peer groups do not engage in any of the negatively oriented delinquent behavior of the other groups. They consider members of such groups "losers" and their behavior "dumb, disgusting, and stupid." A child in such a group therefore is pressured to stay away from the people and behavior of negative groups even though members of the negative groups may call them names such as "brown nosers," "brainers," and "preppies."

Whether children are in a positive group, a negative group, or one in between (which is more often the case), it is important that they be part of some group. Being accepted by peers, being a member of a group, and having friends provide a sense of security at this unstable time in their lives. While they are breaking away from adult dependence, being a member of a group provides them with a sense of influence, a feeling of power, and some recognition of their own value within a social unit outside of the family.

The peer group is the primary source of outside feedback for early adolescents as they try out their new roles in their quest for independence. Thus, early adolescents' status within the group becomes the most important social relationship in their lives. This is followed by their status within the school and within society as a whole. Their status within the family becomes less and less significant during these years.

It is paradoxical that at a time in their lives when early adolescents are trying to discover who they are and to become independent individuals in society, their individuality is continually surrendered to the group in their desire for peer acceptance. The need to conform is greatest during the ages of 12 to 15 and tends to decline afterward.

## THE BEST FRIEND SYNDROME

The "best friend" syndrome also develops during puberty. While having friends is important, having a best friend (especially for girls) is particularly important. The best friend is someone the early adolescent can talk with and confide in on a daily basis, someone with whom to share thoughts, hopes, and worries. While most early adolescents have a best friend, they may change best friends often. At times, girls even compete with one another to become someone's best friend. While associated with a best friend, early adolescents expect complete loyalty from that person. If betrayed by such a friend, early adolescents can become upset and react in a highly emotional fashion. It can also be a blow to the early adolescent ego to be a person's best friend and then be reduced to "second best" friend.

## TWO PERSONALITIES

Because of the need to secure friendships and acceptance of peers, early adolescents quickly discover that it is impossible to please both adults and their friends or peer group. The early adolescent child is often torn between the two as a result. In trying to please both parents and peers, children sometimes assume two personalities: one for the home and one for the peer group. But most children cannot maintain two distinct personalities forever, and eventually the peer group personality begins to surface at home.

In switching allegiance from family to peer group, early adolescents transfer uncompromising authority to the peer group.

Parents are often shocked by the things their children do under the group's influence. Telling lies about where they have been or what they have done is not uncommon, even among the "best raised" and trusted children. For many children, the pressure and influence of the peer group cannot be overestimated. Parents often respond to outsiders' reports of their child's whereabouts and activities with disbelief and denial. For example, a parent has no knowledge that his child smokes because the child does not smoke at home. However, an adult relative may see the child smoking in the company of friends at a mall.

## THE SAMENESS FACTOR

One of the early adolescent's greatest fears is being different in some way from her peers. Therefore, sameness is important during early adolescence. Conformity to the group in terms of mannerisms, dress, speech, behavior, consumerism, music, and other fads is to be expected. Early adolescents want to dress like their friends, behave like their friends, and talk like their friends so that they will be accepted. Early adolescents have a flock mentality. To be different in any way during early adolescence is to be doomed.

Afraid of being different, many early adolescents fear that others will single them out for their differences (for example, having old-fashioned clothes, having a long nose, or speaking with a lisp). As a result, early adolescents often make fun of others as a way of diverting attention away from themselves and their own differences. In doing this, they can be very cruel toward others. Sometimes, a student in a class is singled out by class members, and everyone "picks on" the child. More often than not, the student is a nice, normal child, and there appears to be little legitimate reason for this action. Other times the "picked on" child is different from the other children in some way (for example, overweight or handicapped). For children who become the targets of such behavior, life can become a nightmare. Other children do not want to associate with them for fear of being ridiculed themselves. As a result, many of these children become isolated and eventually become depressed, losing self-confidence because "nobody likes them." This is despite the fact that they are very likable, lovable children. Eventually, a child at the center of such ridicule may not want to go to school. One trait these children have in common is their timidness. They are usually not the type of kids who fight back or stand up to others; therefore, it is easy to pick on them.

The media, especially advertisers, often capitalize on early adolescent vulnerability and the "sameness" factor that characterizes them. They understand the early adolescent mentality and know how to appeal to it just as they know how to appeal to other groups in society. Because they are in the early phases of discovering the world and what it is all about, early adolescents often have trouble discriminating between fantasy and reality. Thus they are easily influenced by fantasy in advertisements.

## SIGNIFICANCE OF BRAND NAMES

Brand name manufacturers spend a significant amount of money advertising their products using the fantasy theme. Early adolescents easily buy into it because brand names are supposed to be the best, associated in commercials and ads with the good life, good times, popularity, sexiness, and prestige. Brand names, of course, are more expensive than common brands.

In selecting consumer goods, especially shoes and clothing, early adolescents identify with brand name items. Once a number of early adolescents have a certain brand name item (for example, jeans or sneakers), others want the same. Parents may buy a child a pair of jeans that appear to be exactly the same as the brand name pair except in price, but because they aren't a particular brand or don't have a particular company logo on it, the child doesn't want it and may refuse to wear it.

This is, once again, because they want to have the same things as their peers and don't want to be different. Early adolescents insist on the expensive brand name items because they are very insecure and unsure of themselves. If they are wearing the most expensive shoes or clothes available, it makes them feel secure because they are wearing the "best" items possible. This means they won't be ridiculed or laughed at by their peers for having "cheap" or inferior goods, which would make them even more self-conscious and insecure. Of course, because early adolescents don't yet work or have responsibility for their finances, the cost factor is not a significant consideration to them. They just want to look good, and wearing the brand name item helps them feel good about themselves.

This is a sore point for parents. Not only are the popular brand names more expensive, but children grow out of their clothes so quickly during puberty. A greater financial burden on the parent is the result. For example, a pair of $100 sneakers for a child will no longer fit in a few months, and the parent must then buy the child another pair. Of course, many adults are very brand name oriented themselves, and this makes it difficult for them to say no to their child's requests for the same.

## FADS

Early adolescents are very susceptible to fads. While relatively short lived, the fads can be in music, clothing, hairstyle, makeup, or anything significant to them. As some early adolescents begin to buy into a fad, others quickly follow. Wanting to look like or be like friends or others in their peer group, they don't want to appear different in their tastes. Early adolescents will therefore lobby their parents to buy them these faddish items as they become popular and available. But fads pass quickly, and new ones emerge. When this happens, the early adolescent begins to lobby all over again.

# 6

# How Social Development Affects Early Adolescent Behavior

Having reviewed the processes involved in early adolescent social development, we turn now to an examination of the effects of social development on early adolescent behavior.

## REJECTING PARENTS AND FAMILY

During early adolescence, criticism of parents is very common. Parents often wonder if they are loved or if they can do anything right. Early adolescents criticize the way their parents dress, the way they speak, the way they comb their hair, the music they like, the car they drive, their skills, their talents, their successes—the list goes on and on. To achieve independence, children have to stop needing their parents. For early adolescents, rejection of parents and other adults is a means of achieving the feeling of independence. Because this rejection is normal during early adolescence, it should not be taken personally. Try to remain calm, cool, and collected during these times, and try not to let hurt feelings turn to anger, bitterness, and resentment. The child's critical attitude does not last forever.

During puberty, resistance to participating in family-oriented activities begins to grow. Staying away from adults and family means achieving independence. No longer interested in traditional family activities, early adolescents are more apt to choose doing things with their friends. As a result, parents often feel rejected and may make comments like "What's the matter with us? Aren't we good enough anymore?" Once again, rejection of adults during early adolescence is normal. It does not occur because parents have done something wrong or because they aren't loved.

In addition to disassociating themselves from their families, early adolescents are often embarrassed to be seen with their parents or family in front of their peers (for example, when shopping at a mall). Young adolescents want to appear as if they are grown up and don't need an adult to walk around with them everywhere. They are afraid their peers will say things like, "Oh look. There's little Robbie shopping with his father. What a sissy (or other derogatory name). He has to have Daddy around to help him." If you take an early adolescent to the movies, and she brings along a friend, they will probably want to sit across the aisle from you or somewhere else in the theater, and that is fine. You can still supervise them while allowing them some independence. Early adolescents may also be embarrassed about your clothes, hairstyle, or mannerisms in front of their peers, so do not be offended if they distance themselves from you at times in the presence of their peers.

Young adolescents can be very hurtful and blunt in what they say to their parents at times. Characteristically, they don't think beforehand about the effects of what they are saying. They act before they think and in this way frequently hurt other people's feelings. Some early adolescents think their parents don't have any feelings. When children don't get their own way about something and are upset, they may say things such as, "If you didn't want (couldn't afford) kids, why did you have them?" or "I didn't ask to be born." At other times, early adolescents will deliberately say things to get parents upset. For example, Erica says to her mother, "Mom, what would you do if I came home pregnant?"

Concerning what they want parents to look and act like, early adolescents are most comfortable with parents who look and act like parents: not too modern, not too old-fashioned, but neat and conservative. Mothers who dress in too modern a fashion or fathers too far out of fashion can cause early adolescents to be embarrassed. They are particularly embarrassed by mothers who wear sexy or revealing clothing. They are also embarrassed by parents who try to "act cool," be like one of them, use teen vocabulary, tell "stupid" jokes (jokes that aren't funny to early adolescents), or flirt with their friends.

Early adolescents despise being yelled at or scolded by their parents when friends are present. This should be avoided and the problem taken care of after the friends leave. Early adolescents also do not like it when parents tell their friends about their bad behavior (for example, "Do you know what Zenia did last night? She . . .").

## BRINGING A FRIEND ALONG

As early adolescents go through puberty, the importance of friendships increases and the importance of the family temporarily decreases. As this happens, early adolescents want to have friends over more often than they have in the past. Early adolescents, especially girls, want to have sleepovers with a group of close friends or one best friend. When family outings are arranged (such as going to a theme park or the beach), they want to bring a friend along. If the friend they want to have along is someone you know and approve of, let the friend be included in your family outings, when appropriate. By socializing with friends in your presence, or under your supervision, you will know where your child is and what she is doing. The friend the child wants to have along is usually a best friend, so it will often be the same person who will be tagging along to various other events.

Your child will probably be invited to participate in her friend's family outings as well, from time to time. Knowing the character of the friend and her family will be helpful in deciding when to allow or encourage it. The period of wanting to have a friend along is most pronounced from ages 12 to 15. After that time, the need tends to decline. Again, the child's interest in friends is not a reflection on you and is not to be interpreted as the child doesn't love you anymore.

## FINDING A ROLE MODEL

Early adolescents need to have a role model, an ideal adult they can look up to or talk with about things. Parents cannot fulfill this role because early adolescents can identify their faults and weaknesses, making their parents less than ideal in their eyes. As a result, early adolescents choose adults who are sufficiently removed from their immediate environment and whose faults and weaknesses are not evident to them. Many parents feel hurt or rejected when they find out that the child is confiding in or getting advice from another adult. Parents feel that because they know the child and love her more than anyone else, they would be best at fulfilling this role. However, this is a temporary situation, and it should not be taken personally. The child may choose a relative, a friend's parents, a neighbor, or a teacher. It is hoped the child will choose someone you know and trust. When you sense that your child is entering this phase, encouraging such a relationship with someone you feel is suitable is probably a good idea. It will decrease the possibility that your child will choose someone with less desirable traits. If the opportunity arises someday, be prepared to play this role for someone else's child. Perhaps you have already had the experience of being the confidant of an early adolescent child in the past as a single adult, as a young parent, or as an older brother or sister of an early adolescent.

## REBELLION

Rebellion is perhaps one of the most difficult characteristics of early adolescence with which adults have to contend. It becomes more pronounced as early adolescents enter the early teen years, and it evokes many negative feelings such as a loss of control and a sense of helplessness and hopelessness on the part of parents. It is important for parents to understand the reasons for early adolescent rebellion. Early adolescents rebel because they need to establish themselves as individuals with their own feelings, values, tastes, and opinions. They have a strong need to prove to themselves, as well as to others, that they have their own minds. Young adolescents rebel against authority in order to feel that they are becoming independent. You cannot stop the child's need to rebel, and you shouldn't try to. It is a psychological need with which early adolescents must deal. It is normal, and it is necessary if the young adolescent is going to achieve independence and an identity of his own.

Rebelling is not a consequence of how a child is raised. Parents often ask themselves questions like, "Where did we go wrong?" or "Why is he doing this to us?" They believe that if the child had been "raised properly," he would not rebel. However, it is abnormal if an early adolescent child does not rebel. All children must go through a period of rebellion sooner or later. Those that don't rebel during early adolescence will do so later in their teens or sometimes as late as their midtwenties. Sometimes the consequences of rebelling later can be worse than those of early rebellion because they may be more difficult to reverse. For example, a girl in her late teens marries a boy her parents disapprove of just to spite them or prove that they are wrong about him. Two years later, the girl has had a child, has quit school, and is in the process of getting a divorce. If you notice that other parents of early adolescents are not having any trouble with rebellion and you are, do not think that your child is rebellious because you have done something wrong and the other parents have done something right. In time, their children will rebel too.

Early adolescent rebellion can manifest itself in two ways. Early adolescents can engage in rebellious acts that do not endanger their safety or health or cause any long-term harm, or they can rebel by doing things that could have long-term negative or destructive effects. Safe ways that early adolescent children rebel include playing music you don't like and playing it loudly, having weird clothes or hairstyles, wearing makeup, having messy rooms, wearing outrageous jewelry, swearing, talking tough, and so on. Harmful or destructive ways to rebel include using drugs or alcohol, having sex, or getting involved in vandalism and crime.

During these years of rebellion, the parents' objective is not to stamp out the rebellion completely, nor the need for independence. Unfortunately, that will probably make the situation worse. Rather, the goal is to confine the rebellious behavior to things that will not cause the child any harm in the long term—to allow her to rebel in safe ways. In this way, the child will fulfill the need to rebel and will suffer few, if any, serious consequences in the long run.

## PEER PRESSURE

When we think about peer pressure, most of us automatically associate the term with negative, deviant acts that children do as a result of pressure from their friends. But as we said earlier, peer pressure does not always result in negative consequences. If the pressure influences children to keep out of trouble, it can be viewed as positive. Peer pressure also results in the standardization of early adolescent behavior. Early adolescents dress in a similar way, have similar hairstyles, have similar tastes in music, and so on. This uniformity results from pressure to be the same as others of the same age group. Not conforming would make a child different and therefore subject to rejection or ridicule.

The peer pressure we fear most, of course, is that which influences children to do things that are dangerous and unsafe or that may cause them long-term harm or suffering. In these circumstances, friends may coerce children into smoking, drinking, stealing, vandalizing, using drugs, or having sex, in order to be accepted. This behavior repeated over time will eventually cause a child to suffer negative and perhaps devastating consequences.

As you observe your early adolescent becoming more peer oriented, it is helpful to discuss peer pressure with him. Talk about what peer pressure is and why it exists. Tell the child that peer pressure is strongest at his age and tell him why. Discuss potential problems before they arise, and provide input as to what the child might say or do in these situations. Examples include the following: What if an adult or friend approaches you with drugs? What if a friend encourages you to smoke or drink? What if a boy pressures you to kiss him or have sex? What if a friend pressures you to go places without letting your parents know? What if a friend pressures you to "pick on" another kid? A child may be confronted with peer pressure at any time, and as a result, she will have to make a split-second decision. If you discuss some potential situations ahead of time, the child will have something to fall back on when the time comes. He will remember what was said during such a discussion and, it is hoped, will do the right thing as a result. Of course, not every child will do the right thing. Some will not be able to resist the pressure of peers. However, those who have not had any opportunity to think about peer pressure and the consequences of becoming involved in negative behavior will have nothing to fall back on. This would make it more difficult for them to resist doing things they wouldn't otherwise do.

The child needs to know that he is not the only one who feels pressure. Many of his friends feel the same pressures too. And, if he would say "no" when pressured to do something he is not comfortable with, others might follow and walk away from the situation with him.

Early adolescents with a good self-concept and positive self-esteem are less prone to peer pressure because they have the confidence to walk away from a situation with which they are not comfortable. They are not afraid of disagreeing with others. Conversely, children who have a negative self-image and poor self-esteem are more easily influenced by peers because they desperately want to be liked and accepted. As a result, they are more likely to conform to peer pressure in order to gain acceptance.

Having a good and trusting relationship with a parent gives a child a better sense of self and more confidence. This, too, serves as a defense against peer pressure. If a hostile relationship exists between parent and child, the child is more likely to turn to her peers for acceptance and is therefore more likely to conform to peer pressures.

## THE INFLUENCE OF FRIENDS

One of the most important influences, if not the most important influence, in the life of an early adolescent child is his friends. If a child associates with friends of questionable character, he will likely engage in negative behavior in order to be accepted and be considered part of the group. By the same token, a child who associates with friends of good character will not likely get involved in negative or harmful behaviors because he will be pressured to stay away from such behaviors. Thus, the type of friends a child has during early adolescence is extremely important. This point should be taken seriously. While parents cannot and should not choose their son's or daughter's friends, they can encourage friendships with children of good influence and character (positive friends) and discourage friendships with children who might lead their child astray (negative friends).

## DEVELOPING POSITIVE FRIENDSHIPS

Attempts to develop a pattern of positive friendships should begin as early as possible, preferably before the arrival of puberty. Establishing a pattern of positive friendships early on will set in place friendships that children will likely continue during early adolescence. Try to steer children away from negative friendships early, before the friendship becomes too strong or serious. Once puberty has arrived and early adolescents have established themselves as part of a group of friends who are always in trouble, although it is not too late to do anything about it, it certainly will not be easy to keep the child away from such friends.

How do you encourage positive friendships? Encourage your child to socialize with friends of good influence and character. Make positive comments to your child when she chooses friends of this type. Encourage your child to invite these friends to your home to socialize, especially new friends. Include your child's friend in family activities and outings when she wants to bring a friend along. While it may be annoying to put up with their music, noise, and giggling, you will at least know where they are, what they are doing, and with whom. If your child brings her friend home, you will also get an opportunity to judge the character of a new friend. If there is an opportunity to talk with your child's friend's parents, take the opportunity to do so in order to get some insight into the child and her background.

Encourage your child to become involved in after-school activities that are arranged and supervised by the school. There, he can socialize in a positive setting with children who are likely to be of a more positive character. Kids that are always in trouble don't usually join the school choir or science club.

## DISCOURAGING NEGATIVE FRIENDSHIPS

If the child begins to socialize with another child of questionable character, try to steer him away from that friend. This works best if it can be done in a subtle way. Don't encourage the friendship. Tell the child that you don't approve of the friend and why. If the child does not give up the friendship, repeat your message from time to time, particularly if an appropriate situation arises in which your message can find some validation. For example, your child waits for a friend to visit, and the friend doesn't arrive and doesn't call to say he won't be coming. The child becomes upset and says, "Where's Nathan? He said he'd be here at 7 o'clock. Why hasn't he come?" At this point, the parent might say something like, "Isn't this the third time that Nathan hasn't shown up while you waited for him? How does it make you feel? I guess Nathan isn't a very reliable friend." It is hoped the child will discontinue the friendship and look for someone more suitable, as he realizes that the friendship is not all that good. If a child persists with a negative friendship and if all else fails, you might try forbidding him to continue the friendship. In the early stages of puberty, this may work. And before puberty, the child will likely comply. However, once in the rebellious phase, forbidding a child to associate with a friend may not work. Because he is being rebellious, he will likely defy you and keep the friendship simply to rebel or to prove you wrong.

## HELPING KIDS WHO ARE "PICKED ON"

Early adolescents often make fun of other kids or chastise and tease them as a way of diverting attention away from themselves, their differences, or their insecurities. As mentioned earlier, often a perfectly normal and pleasant child in a class is singled out and becomes a scapegoat for everyone to pick on. This cruelty is difficult for adults to comprehend, but it is nonetheless typical behavior of early adolescent children. Parents need to encourage their children to avoid becoming involved in this type of behavior.

Acceptance by friends and peers is important to healthy psychological development in early adolescence. If your child is one of the children who is being chastised by fellow classmates for no apparent reason, several things can be done to help the child cope with the situation while meeting the important need for social acceptance and friendships.

Look for opportunities where the child can socialize with other children of the same age in settings outside the school. For example, encourage the child to join a boys/girls club, various local or town-sponsored sports leagues, YMCA/YWCA youth groups, library- or museum-sponsored clubs, or church-organized youth groups. Have the child participate in youth community service projects, or get the child involved in lessons that focus on group instruction (such as ballet, karate, or gymnastics). Early adolescent girls are fond of having penpals in other countries or in different parts of the United States. They can be encouraged to have penpals to whom they can write and share their interests. In these contexts, children are provided with opportunities to social-ize and make friends with other children the same age—children who are unaware that the child is being rejected by classmates in school.

It is important for parents to keep a child's self-esteem intact when the child is faced with this unfortunate behavior in school. Children in these situations can easily come to the conclusion that "nobody likes me." Self-esteem can be reinforced in several ways.

First, the child needs to be repeatedly reassured that there is nothing wrong with her, that the problem is not with her but rather with the children who are ridiculing her. Explain that these chil-dren engage in this behavior because they are insecure and afraid others might tease them. Talk to the child about why kids pick on others at this age. Show her the passage in the previous chapter of this book that addresses this issue to reinforce what you say, if appropriate. Use the positive friendships the child forms outside of the school to reinforce that there is nothing wrong with her.

Encourage the child not to react to the teasing of classmates by becoming upset because that usually leads to even more teasing. Explain that one of the objects of the classmates is to upset her, and when they do that, they feel they have succeeded in their mission. By not becoming upset, by trying to ignore the behavior, and by trying hard to be brave, she will help to avert more attacks in the future. Tell her that if she feels like crying or yelling at them, she should wait until she comes home, and then she can cry and let her frustrations out there with your support.

Alerting the teacher to the problem can also be of help in the event that the teacher is not already aware of it. If the teacher is contacted, however, it must be done discreetly because if the other children find out, it can backfire for the child. They may increase the teasing by saying things such as, "Oh what a big baby . . . Has to have Mommy come and talk to the teacher. Can't stand on her own two feet without Daddy. What are you going to do now? Run home and tell Mommy?" Comments like this can make the child feel even worse.

Assure the child that she is loved and that you are very proud of her. Tell her you think she is a fine young adult, and praise her for her strengths and good qualities and for her ability to be strong and withstand the teasing. You can also discreetly alert older relatives close to the child such as a favorite aunt or older cousin. Tell them about the situation, and ask them to help reinforce her self-esteem at any appropriate opportunity during the troublesome period.

## KEEPING EARLY ADOLESCENTS BUSY

Another way to reduce some of the possible negative effects of peer pressure during early adolescence is to keep early adolescents busy. Encourage them to become involved in after-school clubs, sports teams, and after-school lessons. In these more positive settings, the need to socialize will be satisfied, and at the same time, they may be learning something and having fun. Most of all, they will keep out of trouble. If early adolescents are busy and involved in things, they will not have as much time to get into trouble. Having responsibility for chores around the house can be part of this. When they are old enough, they can also babysit, cut lawns, and so on, as a part-time "job." Early adolescents who are bored or have nothing to do may go looking for trouble. They are more likely to hang around the corner store waiting for friends and looking for something (rebellious) to do with them.

## INSPIRING CONFIDENCE AND SELF-ESTEEM

Do all you can to inspire confidence and self-esteem in a child from a young age. Research demonstrates that the better a child feels about himself and the more confident he is, the less likely he is to be influenced strongly by peers and their demands. The more insecure a child is and the lower his self-esteem, the more he will need to be accepted by the group to prove he is of worth. This results in being more susceptible to peer pressure. In general, if the family has had a strong influence in the child's life until early adolescence, friends will have only a temporary negative influence on the child, if any at all.

## FADS

Early adolescents will be drawn to fads during puberty. Fads are part of the "sameness" factor. Early adolescents want to have the same clothes, speech, and mannerisms as their peers. If one influential child gets something, everyone wants to have it. Parents need not be too concerned about a child having faddish items (for example, clothes), or doing faddish things (for example, wearing shoes with laces undone), as long as the fad does not cause the child any long-term harm. Fads are a normal part of early adolescence, and they usually do not last very long.

## CLOTHING

As for clothing and the brand names that seem to be so popular with early adolescents, once a child reaches puberty, especially the teen years, he should be increasingly allowed to choose much of his clothing within the budget you allocate. This allows early adolescents to make decisions and have an influence on how they will look. It becomes a means of expression of their individuality as well as a way to conform to the styles of their peers. If you don't like the choices she makes (that is, style or color), voice your disapproval and give your reasoning to the child. Unless the child chooses something that is outside of acceptable norms (that is, sexy, revealing, or not appropriate for the function it is intended for), try to allow her the choice. Remember, the child wants to look like everyone else, and if he does not, he may have to suffer the consequences of peer ridicule or nonacceptance. As for expensive brand name items, a certain number of such items could be considered, if possible. If you wish, the child can be asked to pay for part of them, or when older, pay for the difference between what you will allow for an item and the cost of what the child has chosen. Limits can be set according to your personal financial situation as well as your values and beliefs. When buying expensive brand name items, however, the child should be cautioned to make sure it fits and that she likes it. The outlay of a large sum of money may be in vain if the item is discarded shortly after its purchase.

Also, while you might allow your child to wear faddish styles you disapprove of to school, you can ask that he wear more conservative clothing when out with the family (for example, to church or to a wedding). This is a compromise most families can reach.

Another suggestion is that if the child learns to sew and enjoys it, she can learn to make some of her clothing in the latest styles and at a great savings, allowing more money for a greater selection of clothing.

## FANTASY

Because early adolescents' first impressions of adult life and the world are filled with fantasy and not very realistic, it is useful to discuss with them the role of fantasy on television and in movies, videos, and advertisements. Explain that although fantasy serves a role in our lives (that is, it is a good form of entertainment and an escape from routine and problems), what happens on television and in the movies does not happen very often in real life. Some of the myths encouraged by television can be discussed and dispelled. Examples can include the following:

1. Adults' lives aren't as wonderful as you may think they are. Adults have to work because no one gives them money or provides them with a place to live or groceries to eat. They have to get up early and go to work every day whether they like it or not. If the child wants an example of what adults' lives are like, ask him what he thinks of your life (or another relative's life). Tell him that your life is typical of the lives of most adults.

2. People who are attractive, such as models and movie stars, are not always happy. They have problems too. Many are very unhappy, as indicated by the number of them who become depressed, take drugs, commit suicide, and so on. People who are not attractive have happy lives too. They have boyfriends and husbands and jobs like everyone else. Looks aren't everything. Looks may attract people to each other in the beginning, but real friendships go far beyond looks.

3. Everyone is not happy all of the time. That is how life is, and we have to learn to cope with it. We all have problems, and they cannot be solved in a 30-minute time span as portrayed on television. We all have good times, bad times, and in-between times. Sometimes when we are experiencing a bad time, we think it will not end, but it will. Things don't always turn out the way we expect them to, so we have to learn to accept what cannot be changed.

4. To sell beer, advertisers show that people who drink have fun. But that isn't always the case. While drinking in moderation is OK for adults, too much alcohol can have negative effects. Give examples of cases where your child may have seen some of the negative results of drinking. Ask the child questions such as, "Do you think it is nice for

Aunt Mary or the kids when Uncle Stan is drunk and yelling at them all the time? How do you think Mrs. Carmine feels about having lost her only daughter to a drunk driver?"

5. In real life, casual sex is not the norm, and sex is not always expected on dates.
6. Girls who become pregnant don't have physicians and lawyers fighting over them as they do on television.

You can also discuss the role of singers and stars in videos, explaining that the star's goal is to get popular by selling lots of tapes and videos. These stars have to dress differently or provocatively to get attention. If they were nice, conservative girls or boys dressed in formal clothes, and if they stood behind a microphone singing and doing very ordinary things, chances are that no one would notice them or pay any attention to them. So these people dress outrageously and do outrageous things to get attention, to appeal to your sense of fantasy, and to arouse curiosity. Point out to the child that this is done so that people will like the stars and make them popular by buying their videos and musical selections. Tell the child that watching all of these fantasies is OK as long as they realize that they are fantasies and that things don't happen like this very often in real life.

As you discuss the fantasies of adult life and the fantasies of television and the media, some early adolescents will respond by saying things like, "I know they aren't real," while others will probably not believe you at the time and may not accept what you say or may argue with you about it. However, overtime, as they have to deal with the disappointments that their fantasies and idealism bring, they will remember what you said, and it will help them deal with the disappointment a little better.

The best time to discuss these things is when a related opportunity arises or when the situation lends itself to doing so. Then it seems a natural extension of your conversation or the circumstances rather than an isolated event discussed out of context.

# DISCUSSING THE ROLE OF ADVERTISING

Discussing the role of advertising and advertisers with early adolescents is also useful. Explain that advertisers are trying to draw attention to a product. To do this, they tell people about all the good things the product does or can do. They also use fantasy to convince people that products will make them happy in one way or another. Point out that many advertisements are unrealistic and contain much fantasy to entice people to buy the product. However, advertisers don't have too much choice in the way they portray their products. To illustrate why this is the case, ask the child if she would buy soap or shampoo that didn't claim to be the best. Or would she buy jeans that were advertised on an overweight model or makeup modeled by someone with an unattractive face? We can advise early adolescents to view advertisements with skepticism, and we can tell them not to believe their messages before examining them critically. Early adolescents need to be cautioned to stop and think about the claims being made about a product and whether the claims are realistic.

# 7

# Intellectual Development

In recent decades, much has been discovered and learned about the intellectual development of children. As of yet, however, no theory, study, or research has produced an absolutely clear or definitive picture of human mental development in which development and age, for example, can be matched exactly. However, general characteristics that correspond to certain ages in children have been identified in many independent research studies with similar findings. Considering the work of researchers as it relates to intellectual development during the early adolescent years, we will now examine some general characteristics of the early adolescent intellect and mental development.

## THE CHANGING
## EARLY ADOLESCENT INTELLECT

The most significant characteristic of the early adolescent intellect is its changing nature. Not only are early adolescents changing physically, biologically, emotionally, and socially, as we have already seen, but they are changing intellectually as well. As they begin puberty, early adolescents' thinking capabilities and mental abilities are more like those of a child. During puberty, however, the intellectual nature of a child undergoes transformation and becomes more like that of an adult. Thus, early adolescents are in a transitional intellectual state between child-like (concrete) thinking and adult-like (formal) thinking.

## CONCRETE THINKING

When a child begins puberty, he is more of a concrete thinker. A child in the concrete thinking stage organizes information around concepts, categories, or things that are visible and identifiable. There is a need for concrete referents. For example, children must see objects of differing sizes in order to discriminate the differences between them. They are not able to visualize differences in sizes as adults do. They cannot think about something being 12 meters (40 feet) wide. They must see it in front of them in order to visualize it. Children need direct contact with ideas, things, events, situations, and people in order for these things to be represented in their minds. They can use logic, but only to achieve solutions of simple problems of a concrete nature. As concrete thinkers, children have fairly rigid patterns of thinking. They also think mainly in terms of "the here and now" and are unable to visualize and project alternatives and possibilities into the future.

## FORMAL THINKING

As a child progresses through early adolescence and toward the mid-teen years, she begins to develop the intellectual characteristics of an adult and becomes more of a formal thinker. Formal thinking is adult-like thinking. It is characterized by the ability to think about things and form ideas about things that are not directly visible. Formal thinkers are able to visualize, conceptualize, hypothesize, and reason, and they can think in the abstract at an optimal level. The development of formal thinking represents the final stage of intellectual development in humans. It is final in that formal thinking is potentially the highest level of thinking possible. When formal thinking develops, children begin to think in terms of general principles, without the need for concrete or visible referents. As this happens during puberty, a whole new world opens up to the early adolescent. He can now extend his mental world by projecting possibilities and alternatives, and he can see possible implications of actions. With formal thinking, early adolescents develop a sense of perspective and time. They can visualize historical events and, through reason, understand how and why they occurred. The thinking in the "here and now" that characterized the childhood years expands to a world of possibilities and hypotheses. Early adolescents begin to think about and visualize alternatives to things they couldn't see or imagine before. They also use more adult-like forms of information processing and problem solving to do so. As they become formal thinkers, early adolescents also begin to separate their personal viewpoints from those of others.

As a result of the movement from concrete thinking to formal thinking, most early adolescent children are in an in-between state of intellect. They are old enough and have developed enough to go beyond the child-like thinking that characterized childhood, but they have not yet fully mastered adult-like thinking. Their minds are in a transitional and fluctuating state somewhere in between. They sometimes react mentally using child-like thinking patterns, while at other times, they use more adult-like methods. At still other times, they use a combination of both.

## VARIABILITY IN MENTAL GROWTH AND DEVELOPMENT

As in other areas of development, early adolescent children progress through the transition from concrete thinking to abstract thinking at different times and rates. Variability between and within specific mental abilities over time is common among early adolescents. Because individual growth rates are variable, we cannot predict exactly when a child actually begins developing formal thinking processes. Rarely does a child think formally before the age of 11 or 12.

Early adolescents acquire formal thinking skills gradually at their own rate over time. Research indicates that by age 14, only about one-quarter of them reach a level of formal thinking. However, the two-year period from age 14 to 16 represents the optimal time for the brain to develop formal thinking. During this time, formal thinking is established and stabilized in the majority of students who are able to reach this level of thinking. This base of skills will then be matured and refined into adulthood. Some students are unable to reach this level of thinking as a result of poor nutrition, damage from drug use, brain dysfunction, a general lack of ability, and various other reasons. It appears, then, that while formal thinking develops during early adolescence, the optimal level is reached during the 14 to 16 age period.

It is important to note that while formal thinking skills may be present in children during early or late adolescence, it does not mean that they are capable of demonstrating formal thinking and reasoning in all subject areas and in all situations. Abilities can vary from subject area to subject area and from circumstance to circumstance.

## SLOWDOWN IN INTELLECTUAL GROWTH

Another characteristic of early adolescent intellect that emerges from research is that there appears to be a slowdown in intellectual growth and mental capacity between ages 12 and 14. This begins somewhat earlier in girls than in boys, and it generally corresponds to children in the seventh and eighth grades. During this period of time, most children are not able to learn as much or as quickly as they did before. From ages 14 to 16, when most children acquire and develop the adult thinking processes that they will carry with them for life, intellectual growth seems to increase again. While there are theories to explain this phenomenon, research is ongoing.

## EFFECTS OF OTHER DEVELOPMENTAL CHANGES ON INTELLECT

While the rate of mental growth and development varies from child to child, early adolescent mental attitude and growth is often influenced by various other developmental changes occurring simultaneously (for example, biological, physical, social, and emotional). Shorter attention spans, increased restlessness, and unstable emotions that result from changing biology, as well as increasing social pressure, can influence mental outlook, interest, and effort put forth by early adolescent students. For example, under strong peer pressure and the desire to be accepted by the group, some students deliberately do poorly on tests and assignments so that they will not be seen as different, or smarter, by others in the group or class, thereby avoiding rejection and labeling.

As we discussed earlier, socialization and friends are usually the focal point of the lives of most early adolescent children. Academics are not always a priority, and so some early adolescents do not put as much effort into school work and learning as they might. Because early adolescents are somewhat egocentric in how they view the world and their environment, they consider much of what they are taught in school as irrelevant, unimportant, and boring. This is mainly because they see no practical reason for learning it. Having them see some relevance or applicability in the here and now can help to overcome this thinking.

## IDEALISM

Another important characteristic of the early adolescent intellect is its idealistic nature. As a result of the development of adult thought processes during puberty, early adolescents are very vulnerable to idealism during these years. Because they can now think in terms of possibilities, anything imaginable to early adolescents seems possible. Being in the early stages of adult thinking, most early adolescents have not yet developed beyond this level to determine whether their ideas are realistic or workable in reality. When thinking of possibilities, they dwell on perfection. This is why early adolescents so often offer ideal solutions to complex problems, and idealistic alternatives and endings to various life situations. The expression of idealism is very strong during early adolescence because their thought processes lack the ability to make the connection between what they think and what is reality.

## OTHER INTELLECTUAL CHARACTERISTICS

There are other characteristics of the early adolescent intellect. Early adolescents love to experiment and explore. Just as they do this in their search for independence and an identity of their own, they can do so in learning situations. Early adolescents generally have vivid imaginations and thus can be very creative, generating innovative work and projects as a result. However, they do need encouragement in this area because their tendency toward self-consciousness and a lack of self-confidence can hold them back.

Early adolescent attention spans and concentration levels alter during puberty, becoming temporarily shorter than in previous periods. They cannot concentrate for long periods of time and need to break up learning situations into smaller chunks of time.

Preferring to be actively involved in mental activities rather than participate as observers, early adolescents like to roll up their sleeves and get involved in learning situations rather than sit and listen to a lecture.

Early adolescents are also curious individuals. The learning they enjoy most is that which relates to their current interests and goals. They will work hard to achieve goals they see as worthwhile.

In their search for their own identity, early adolescents often ponder the meaning of life from intellectual, philosophical, social, and ethical points of view. As early adolescents begin to philosophize about life, they enjoy having discussions with adults about their experiences. Although early adolescents can evaluate issues critically, they are not always objective in their evaluations. They often support the underdog's point of view or take the opposing point of view in a conversation or debate. They argue to clarify personal thinking as much as to convince others.

During puberty, early adolescents begin to see people for what they are. They can detect insincerity in others. Adults are no longer able to pull the wool over their eyes as they begin to see through people and situations on their own. Early adolescents are often insulted by adults who try to fool or outwit them, or who underestimate their intellectual skills.

## THE MIDDLE SCHOOL

Most early adolescents in the United States today attend a middle school for their education. Middle schools can also be known as intermediate, senior public, or junior high schools. They usually include a range of three or four consecutive grades from as low as the fourth grade to as high as the ninth. States and school districts vary in their choice of the grade range to include in their middle schools. The most common grade arrangements in American middle schools at present are those that include grades 6 through 8 or grades 5 through 8. Middle schools that include grades 7 through 9 are also common. While middle schools are now found in other countries (for example, Canada), the middle school concept was created in the United States.

As early as 1900, when educators began to realize that early adolescent children were a unique group, they developed the idea of a separate school for children between the elementary and secondary years (early adolescent children). Early adolescents do not have the characteristics of elementary aged children, nor do they have the characteristics of high school students. As we have discussed throughout this book, during the 10- to 14-year age period, early adolescents are undergoing tremendous physical, biological, emotional, social, and intellectual changes. In the midst of experiencing these changes, early adolescents are no longer children but are not yet young adults. They are in a stage of life somewhere in between the two.

The elementary school was developed around certain concepts or principles that relate to the development of the child as a whole. The elementary school is characterized by self-contained classrooms, where one teacher teaches all subjects to the same students in the same room every day. The classroom of students is like a second family to the child. Students know each other well, and the teacher knows the students on a one-to-one basis. The teacher in an elementary school serves a quasi-parental role, helping students with social and emotional development in addition to intellectual development.

The high school is developed around the concepts and principles related more to adults. The high school is characterized by teachers who are subject-area specialists. Students move from room to room during the course of the day, and they encounter different teachers and different students in each class. Teachers do not get to know students well because they have anywhere from 90 to 150 students to deal with during the day. The teacher's role in high school is mainly academic.

Early adolescent children do not belong in either of these settings. They are too old for one and not old enough for the other. Because of the constant changes they are experiencing, early adolescents need a school setting that will meet the unique needs and characteristics of children in this transitional state. The purpose of the middle school is to provide a transitional place between elementary and high school by combining elements from both of these areas to make school as appropriate and comfortable as possible for the early adolescent individual.

The middle school movement toward housing early adolescent children in separate schools away from elementary or high schools was slow to develop from the 1900s to the 1960s and 1970s. Since then, however, the growth has been tremendous. The result is that the majority of early adolescent children in the United States today attend middle schools.

It is important to recognize that contrary to what many people believe, the middle school is not a mini high school. The middle school and the middle school curriculum are designed to meet the unique characteristics and special needs of the changing nature of the early adolescent student. The middle school has a philosophy of its own, and that philosophy underlies all that is done at the middle school level.

## Characteristics of a Middle School

What are the characteristics of the middle school, and what are its advantages over a kindergarten to 12th grade setting or a 6th to 12th grade arrangement? Incorporating some of the elements of both the elementary and high schools, middle schools have certain traits in common. In most middle schools, students have a homeroom and a homeroom teacher who gets to know the students on an individual basis through daily in-depth contact. The purpose of the homeroom is to promote more intense involvement and communication between teacher and student. This provides students with a sense of roots and belonging so that they don't feel they are just another number or just another face in the crowd, as is often the case in the high school. A homeroom period is usually scheduled as a 20- to 30-minute period at the beginning or end of the school day. During this period, announcements are made and students work on homework or study skills, plan field trips, do projects, have a reading period, and do many other things. This gives teachers an opportunity to get to know, on an individual basis, a manageable number of students in a meaningful way. The child, therefore, has an adult who can support him in social or emotional development as well as with administrative or academic tasks or problems. The homeroom period and home-room teacher are part of the familiar elementary school concept transported to the middle school setting. For the rest of the day, students rotate to various classes for separate subject areas. This prepares them for the high school setting. The student's home-room teacher often teaches her a subject at some point in the day, making the contact with the student even more frequent.

The middle school contains more sophisticated and appropri-ate on-site facilities for subject areas such as science, art, music, and family studies (that is, home economics and shop) that are not available in the traditional kindergarten to eighth grade setting. In the K–8 school, there usually aren't enough students at the sixth to eighth grade levels in a given school to warrant the purchase of specialized equipment and the construction of specialized class-rooms. However, with all of the students in the middle school being in these grades, the use of specialized equipment and facilities is maximized. Middle schools are also better equipped to accommodate the variations in students' physical size by provid-ing desks and equipment in a variety of sizes.

Discipline problems tend to increase during the middle school years as a result of early adolescent behavior (that is, rebellion and defiance). A teaching and administrative staff expe-rienced in working with early adolescent children are better equipped to handle this type of student behavior effectively. School rules developed to control behaviors can also be estab-lished and applied uniformly to all students in the school. This is difficult to do in a K–8 setting because rules suitable for younger children may not be appropriate for older children.

Most teachers in the middle school are trained to work with early adolescents and are aware of their characteristics and the changes they are undergoing. They understand early adolescent behavior and are prepared to deal with the difficult behaviors of these students. Early adolescents are rebelling against adults. Parents bear the brunt of early adolescent rebellion and negative behavior as a result. But teachers are also adults and therefore not exempt from such behavior. Teaching middle school students is a very stressful job for this reason. While parents may have to cope with one or two early adolescents on a daily basis, middle school teachers work with several classes of 30 students. Good classroom management techniques and disciplinary skills are a must for middle school teachers. They must also be patient and resilient in order to withstand the barrage of criticism, negative comments, and rebellion they face from early adolescent students every day. A sense of humor is also a desirable attribute. Most middle school teachers enjoy working with early adolescents and like the challenge that teaching early adolescents presents. More than 50 percent of states in the United States now require specific teacher training and separate certification for middle-level teaching positions. This trend seems to be continuing.

In addition to teachers experienced in working with early adolescent children, guidance counselors, social workers, administrators, school nurses, school psychologists, and other support personnel knowledgeable about the problems and concerns specific to this age group are available and usually on site in the middle school to assist students during these transitional years.

## *The Middle School Curriculum*

The curriculum in a middle school is developed to meet the intellectual characteristics and needs of the early adolescent student. It serves as a transitional one between the elementary and high school curriculum, combining elements from both. The middle school curriculum extends common subject matter and basic skills begun at the elementary level as well as basic knowledge and skills that form the core of subject matter and skills to be developed and expanded at the high school level.

The middle school curriculum includes material in several basic areas of academic and personal development, including knowledge, skill development, attitude development, and the development of the physical self through classes such as physical education and health. Traditional elementary school subject areas such as math, English/reading, science, and social studies are part of the curriculum, but there are usually a few subjects such as family studies and computer studies that are new to the students.

An important goal of the middle school is to foster the development of the emerging intellectual abilities of the early adolescent. This is achieved not only by working with academic subject matter but by developing skills and processes that combine elements of the concrete thinking mode with simple elements of formal thinking. Skills that lend themselves well to the transitional nature of the early adolescent intellect include study skills and information processing skills. Learning study and note-taking skills, the art of discussion and debate, skills of inquiry, and how to research and work with information involves elements of both concrete and formal thinking. Middle school students have to learn how to study independently and how to continue learning on their own. They need to develop an understanding of how knowledge is structured and how to find it in order to work successfully with it in the future.

Learning these skills prepares students with a base of skills that is important for successful learning at the high school and college levels. There they are expected to be more independent, to take their own notes, to research their own topics and information for projects and assignments, and to study from their own notes for tests. The more successfully a student can master these skills at the middle level, the better equipped she will be for success at the high school level and beyond. Research demonstrates that learners need to practice skills extensively in order to master them. Mastery of one skill enables them to advance to a higher level of skill development. When skills are not practiced and mastered, the ability to use them proficiently may be lost.

In the development of new thought processes, early adolescents also begin to engage in rational, critical, and analytical thought patterns at a basic level. In addition, they learn the basics of synthesizing thought and information and begin to use multifaceted logic.

The middle school curriculum also emphasizes the development of social skills and the fostering of emotional development in students, which is not a significant part of the high school curriculum. Opportunities are provided for the development of social skills such as leadership, cooperation, responsibility, and sportsmanship. Group work is often part of daily school activities wherein these goals can be practiced and achieved. Also included in middle school curriculum are opportunities for ethical and moral development as well as aesthetic appreciation (for example, of art and music).

 8

# What to Expect of Early Adolescents Intellectually

What can be expected of children academically during the early adolescent years? If a child has had a steady record of progress throughout the elementary years, he should continue along in about the same way during early adolescence. As is the case with everything else during puberty, however, each child varies in the time and rate at which mental and intellectual development progresses. While some early adolescents will excel during the middle school years, early adolescence is not generally known as a time of great academic strides in children. Most children, therefore, will have to work hard at maintaining the level of achievement they had reached before the middle school years. A significant number of students may fall a notch below their previous performance, and others may do poorly during these years. This does not necessarily mean that those who slip cannot recover. With effort and the passage of time, most will.

## FACTORS THAT NEGATIVELY AFFECT
## SCHOOL PERFORMANCE

There are several common factors that can negatively affect academic performance during the middle years, and most relate to developmental changes in one way or another. First, a number of early adolescents do not do as well academically during their first year of middle school (which may be as early as the fifth grade in some districts) because of the newness of the educational setting. They are unable to get themselves organized for each class and have difficulty adjusting to being responsible for more things on their own without a teacher watching or guiding them every step of the way, as is often the case in elementary school. For a time, the disorientation these students experience can negatively affect school work. As they grow accustomed to the new setting and develop better organizational skills, things tend to improve. If the child appears to be having a problem, talk to her and to her homeroom teacher or the school counselor in order to pinpoint specific problems and to identify ways to help the child adjust to the middle school setting.

A number of children who have done well academically up to the seventh and eighth grade levels may experience a slight drop in grade point averages and performance during these grades. This can be attributed to a slowdown in learning capacity at ages 12 to 14 as well as shorter attention spans and shorter concentration levels. If a child in this position is putting forth the same amount of time and effort into his school work, this slight drop need not be a cause for concern. It can, however, be a frustrating time for the child who does not understand why he is putting in the same effort as usual and not getting the same results. Offering reassurance to the child can be helpful. He can be told that he is developing new thinking skills, and until he gets used to it, things might be a little more difficult and confusing than usual. Encourage him to keep up the effort because it will eventually pay off.

Because mental development varies from child to child, some students may be temporarily overchallenged in one or more subject areas by a curriculum that requires skills and new ways of thinking that a child may not have yet developed to the required degree. The curriculum is generally set for the "average" student. Because each child develops at his or her own pace, an individual child may not be keeping pace with the average or majority in one particular subject area or in many. Therefore, the student may not be able to work successfully with the curriculum for a period of time. For example, a child may be asked to analyze something. While she listens to the teacher explaining how to analyze something, she seems to follow the steps involved. But she may not really grasp what analyzing is at this point. She may just be following the steps outlined by the teacher rather than really understanding or internalizing the processes involved. As a result, she may not do well with a curriculum that requires a lot of analysis. If the child has done well academically to this point in time, this should not be a great cause for concern. The child may be a late developer intellectually and in time will catch up and catch on. Some remediation could be helpful in some situations until this happens. Remember, because a child has become developed physically does not mean that she has also developed intellectually. Development varies from child to child.

Some children do not do as well academically for a time during the middle school years because they are too overwhelmed and preoccupied with all of the changes they are experiencing physically, emotionally, and socially, which makes it difficult for them to concentrate or be focused on school work. This is especially the case if a child is ahead of, or lagging behind, his peers in physical development. The child may spend so much time worrying about what others will say or think, or he may be so preoccupied in thinking about ways to hide or accelerate his development or about how to avoid ridicule, that he can scarcely focus on academics. In this case, students of this type will do less well than they are capable of, not because of any lack of ability, but because they are not focused and are not paying attention during class as a result of their preoccupations. These children need encouragement and constant reassurance about their physical development.

Some students are more interested in the social aspects of

school during early adolescence and thus do not put as much effort as they should into doing well academically. They need to be encouraged to exert more effort. Also, some early adolescents feel pressured to do poorly or not as well as they could, in order to fit in better with peers and so they won't be seen as different by others. In this case, peer pressure needs to be discussed with the child because it, and not a lack of ability, is the underlying problem.

Finally, a small number of children will not do well academically during the middle school years because they are heavily involved in negative behaviors for any number of reasons, including social and emotional problems, involvement with drugs and or crime, or friendships with the wrong crowd. These students are often very defiant and rebellious, refusing to cooperate in class, ignoring assignments, and being generally disruptive. Some of these students tend to miss school regularly, and when they are in school, they are tuned out to what is going on. They are frequently in trouble with teachers or administrators for bad behavior. When a child reaches this point, professional help is needed to uncover underlying problems, to deal with the negative behaviors, and to try and turn the child around before conditions deteriorate even further. School psychologists and counselors are available for this purpose. Mental health professionals in private practice such as psychologists, psychiatrists, and social workers who specialize in the problems of children and adolescents may also be of some help.

If a child is not keeping pace with his usual academic performance during the middle school years, the reason is probably due to one of the factors we have just described rather than to a learning disability. In the majority of cases, learning disabilities and other types of problems have already been identified by the time a student reaches the middle grades. It is possible, however, for a learning disability to have gone undetected. In the event that the child is tested and determined to have a learning disability, help is available through remedial and special education programs. Again, school psychologists, social workers, and counselors are available in most schools to deal with most types of problems encountered by early adolescents. If you are in doubt about any problem or any aspect of your child's learning ability at any time, seek advice and help from a professional. It is much better to be informed or reassured than it is to be constantly worrying about whether something is wrong or about whether you are doing the right things for the child.

## AVOIDING UNREALISTIC DEMANDS

It is hoped that your child will be able to maintain or improve her previous academic performance during the middle years. If this is not the case, however, don't panic. During the middle school years, encourage your child to do well academically, as always, but avoid making unrealistic demands. Early adolescents are under a lot of pressure during puberty because of developmental changes and peer pressure and so on. As we said earlier, they usually will have to work quite hard to maintain previous levels of performance. If a child's performance is down just slightly, do not be too concerned. If it is down significantly, try to determine the reason and deal with it accordingly. When there is an underlying problem (such as peer pressure or lack of organizational skills), and it is dealt with, academics usually improve.

## APPLYING PRESSURE WHEN IT IS NEEDED

If a child is doing poorly because of a lack of effort, some pressure needs to be applied, and his priorities need to be refocused, by whatever means are appropriate. However, pressuring a child who is already overwhelmed with too many other problems, without dealing with those problems, can have negative effects and may push the child to his limit of endurance. In these cases, out of sheer frustration, the child may give up on everything. Early adolescents should be challenged academically but not overloaded. Parents are the best judge of how far to push the child and how to deal with the child's behavior in this regard based on knowledge of the child's personality and previous performance.

## GETTING A CALL FROM THE SCHOOL

There is another point worth mentioning about the middle school years. Don't be surprised if you get a call from the school about a problem with your child, especially a child in the seventh and eighth grades. This is particularly applicable to a child who has been well-behaved and done well academically until this point in time. Peer pressure or the pressures of the changes they are experiencing may cause otherwise good or well-behaved children to act in a negative manner during early adolescence. This can range from engaging in "acting-out" behavior to deliberately doing poorly on tests and exams in order to be accepted by peers.

Parents who have never received calls from the school regarding a problem with their child often react with shock and even denial. Typical reactions include, "Louise never got a C in reading before. The teacher must not be any good" or "Larry has never had any behavior problems before. Someone must have really provoked him." Although these parental statements may hold validity, it would be wise to consider the circumstances carefully before accusations or allegations are made. Remember that early adolescents are under pressure to conform to their peers. As a result, they sometimes develop two personalities, one for the home and their parents and another for their friends and school. As a parent you may not be aware of your child's "school/friend" personality until an incident, such as a call from the school, occurs and brings it to your attention. You can discuss the matter with your child and the teacher or school officials. Then deal with the problem based on your judgment of the situation once you have a clear picture of what has transpired.

Do not hesitate to call or visit your child's school or meet with a teacher or principal if you have questions or problems about any aspect of your child's education or school policy. Take the opportunity to question educators about areas such as school curriculum, school policy, school programs, behavior codes, and so on.

## HOMEWORK

Although some early adolescents may need reminders to complete homework assignments from time to time, middle school students should be in the process of becoming more responsible for doing their homework on their own. Early adolescent students need to learn to work on their own without constant reminders. It is part of becoming independent and taking responsibility for their own actions. If they do not meet these responsibilities, they will have to learn to face the consequences. These consequences are those they will face from the school and teachers as well as those you may impose as a parent. While parents can certainly assist children with homework or help them study for tests, middle school children should learn to become more and more responsible for their own learning as time goes on.

# Managing Early Adolescent Behavior

Parenting early adolescents is not always an easy task. In fact, parents are likely to find this to be the most difficult and stressful period of parenthood. Before the onset of puberty, parents are generally quite happy with their children, because children are more likely to conform to parental views and expectations. However, when children reach puberty and begin to experience rapid changes in all areas of their growth and development, it inevitably begins to affect the way they think and act. Their reaction to the process of growing up and becoming physically mature results in the kinds of behavior typically labeled as rebellious, defiant, inconsiderate, smart-mouthed, moody, irritable, changeable, impulsive, critical, and "too big for their britches." When changes occur and these behaviors start to surface, parents begin to doubt and question their parenting skills and abilities. Parents typically make comments like, "Why won't she listen to me? He doesn't love me anymore. What's wrong with her? How can he do this to me? What am I doing wrong?" In an attempt to look for reasons for the changes in behavior they see in their children, they seldom attribute the behavior change to the child's developmental changes. In most cases, the behavioral changes in early adolescents are simply the result of the developmental changes they are experiencing. For this reason, it is important that parents of early adolescent children become familiar with the process of puberty. When parents understand what these developmental changes are, and how early adolescent behavior is affected by them, they can learn to work and cope with the behaviors more successfully, more confidently, and with less frustration and guilt. Having said that, however, even with an understanding of early adolescent development, it must be recognized that working with early adolescents is seldom easy.

## DELAYED REWARDS OF PARENTING

Parenting an early adolescent often feels like a thankless job—an all give and no take situation. Like other parents of early adolescent children, you at times may feel that you are fighting a losing battle. Your child has "changed" and doesn't want to listen to you anymore. You seem to be making many sacrifices for a child who appears unappreciative and ungrateful of your efforts. At times, you wonder if you can do anything right. Your child seems to be forever criticizing you and almost everything you do. While your child begins to disassociate herself from you more and more, you begin to feel hurt, unloved, and not needed anymore. And while you lie awake in bed at night worrying about whether you are doing the right things for your child or about where you have "gone wrong," you begin to have visions of the terrible way you think your child may turn out. In times like these, the joys and rewards of parenthood have become a faint memory. These reactions and thoughts are very typical of parents of early adolescent children, especially if the early adolescent is the first child in the family to experience puberty.

Unfortunately, most of the rewards of parenting during early adolescence are postponed. The results of all of the time, effort, sacrifices, and hard work invested in parenting during the early adolescent years will not likely be evident until this period is over. To cope with parenthood during your child's early adolescent years, therefore, it is best to take a long-range view regarding the outcome of your efforts. Expect to work hard during this time for results that will not be immediately evident. The results, however, will come in time and will definitely be worthwhile.

## PATIENCE AND PERSISTENCE

Try to be patient and persist with the struggles during early adolescence. The extra time and effort spent during these years will pay off in the long run. Don't expect too much appreciation, gratitude, or recognition from your child during these years. There will certainly not be enough, but it will come when the child is older. When early adolescence is over, you will look back at the difficult period not only with relief, but with a sense of pride for having successfully brought your child through the most difficult and traumatic period of human development. When the child is older, she will be grateful to you for all the things you did and will realize that you did things in her best interests. Of course, the ultimate acknowledgment and tribute of appreciation usually comes once your child has children of her own.

That is not to say that you will not get any pleasure out of parenting an early adolescent child. There will be many moments when you will feel proud and happy. However, these moments are easy to take and don't cause concern. What does cause concern are the worrisome and unhappy times that can trouble you on a day-to-day basis. That is the reason for the focus on negative aspects of early adolescent behavior in this book.

As you struggle with parenting your early adolescent, it is helpful to think back to your own early adolescence. What do you think about how you behaved toward your parents then? Did you give them a hard time? Aren't you glad that they said "no" as many times as they did and that they had your best interests at heart? If you are like most people, you probably feel bad or even guilty about the way you talked to your parents or the way you treated them during your early adolescent years, especially when you recognize the difficulties you may have caused them when they were trying to do their best.

## PARENTING TECHNIQUES

With regard to which parenting techniques are successful and which should be used with children during the early adolescent years, each child is different and each parent is different. There are no easy answers or simple solutions. If there were, we would all be using them with success every day. But although there are no foolproof methods of discipline or behavior management to use with early adolescents, there are some general guidelines and methods that seem to work well most of the time with most children. The suggestions that follow in this chapter have been used successfully by many parents, teachers, and others who work with early adolescents. With the knowledge you have of your child's personality, consider your values and beliefs. Then, using your own parenting style, you can approach the management of your child's behavior using these guidelines as a framework. Once again, for any serious problems (such as destructive, violent, or ungovernable behavior, involvement with drugs or crime, depression, suicidal thinking, or anorexia) or for those that cannot be successfully dealt with, professional help should be sought.

## ADJUSTING YOUR PARENTING STYLE

During a child's early adolescence, most parents will have to make changes to their parenting style. Before a child reaches puberty, parents generally use the "authority and control" model of behavior management to control their child's behavior. As a parent, you are the authority and you use your authority to control your child's behavior. Before age 10, children generally accept and recognize parental authority in controlling their behavior. The parent tells the child to do something and expects it to be done. If the child does not comply, he is punished. This behavior management style is fairly straightforward, and parents use it regularly and efficiently to control a child's behavior.

During early adolescence, however, adhering strictly to authority to control behavior no longer works as well as it once did. As a child becomes more adult-like in appearance and thinking, she wants to be treated more like an adult. Parents of early adolescents have to begin to use authority and control less frequently and begin to make more use of compromise. As the parent, of course, you are still the authority. However, you have to act less "bossy" and act more like an adviser or negotiator. While still maintaining your authority, you have to listen, discuss, and compromise more with your child whenever it is possible or appropriate. Guiding and showing is what is needed rather than telling and ordering. This approach is much more time consuming to implement than the authority and control model. For this reason, parents can become impatient and frustrated with it at times. However, the results achieved using this style are worthwhile.

Parents of early adolescents who use authority and control exclusively to control a child's behavior end up constantly battling the child and may eventually alienate him. In the opposite situation, when parents use little control and allow children to do as they please (because it is too difficult, inconvenient, or troublesome to deal with the situation, or they can't be bothered), they lose control of the child completely. In these situations, more often than not, the child becomes the ruler of the household. It is important to recognize that children at this age develop a disrespect for adults who can no longer control them (including teachers, parents, police, school administrators). They will test the patience and tolerance of these people to the limit.

There are times, of course, when you need to use authority and control. When the circumstances are important enough, you want to "come down hard" on the child to impress on him the seriousness of the matter and your unwillingness to tolerate the behavior. However, if you act like a dictator and use authority and control all of the time for every little thing, the child will feel boxed in with no room to move, and resentment will grow. In fact, the child may grow to resent you so much that he will give up on everything that pleases you and will purposely do the opposite of what you want him to do just to spite you. Thus, during early adolescence, you want to loosen the reins and allow some space and some room for compromise, especially on matters of minor importance.

During the early adolescent years, when your child makes a request of you, listen to the request and think about it until you are ready to give your answer. If you cannot answer the child immediately, tell her you will have to think about it for a while or discuss it with your spouse. Consider your answer as carefully as you can, as circumstances permit, so that when a decision is made, you can stick to it.

There are times when you will say yes and times when you will say no. If you say no, give your reasons or rationale, whether the child appears to accept it or not. If you have thought about your answer carefully and you said no, be firm. Consistency is important in dealing with early adolescents. If you say no frequently and then change your mind, the child will argue and plead with you every time you say no because she knows you probably don't mean no when you say no.

At times, you may, of course, say yes, in which case the child will be happy with your decision. On other occasions, the answer may be yes *and* no, which is part of the compromising nature of managing behavior during these years. For example, your daughter wants to go to the mall with her girlfriend after dinner. She informs you that they intend to walk there and back. You feel that going to the mall is OK, but you don't like the idea of her walking home in the dark. Instead of telling her she can't go, tell her you don't mind her going to the mall, but you don't like the idea of her walking home in the dark. So, if she would like to go to the mall, you will pick her up when she is ready to come home.

Try to cut down on saying no all the time, particularly before you have heard the child's request. You may need to say no, but wait until you hear the whole request before doing so. Early adolescents become very frustrated and feel you are not being fair when the answer is no before they are able to finish the request or sentence.

In summary, then, what is called for during these years is a balance between parental warmth and firmness. Listen to children's requests; consider their needs, feelings, and views; and make a decision in their best interests. Compromise whenever you can on less serious matters, and use authority and control in more serious matters. A certain amount of rebellion and defiance is to be expected. It should be kept in check and not allowed to degenerate to a point where it becomes damaging or uncontrollable.

## CONSIDERING THE CHILD'S BEST INTERESTS FIRST

Do what is right for the child. Do not base your judgment on what the child says his friends are doing. Early adolescents often feel that their peers have more privileges than they actually do. They can be misled by peers who may exaggerate their privileges to look "cool" (for example, "My mother lets me stay out until midnight on week nights"). Of course there will always be one or two kids whose parents let them do anything for whatever reason. What they do should not be considered if the child's request is inappropriate.

Needless to say, your child will not always be happy with your decisions. You can tell the child that it would be easier for you to give in to her wishes and get her "off your back," but you are thinking of her best interests. And because you are, you have to do what's right.

Surprisingly, you may do your child a favor by saying no. The child may find it difficult to say no to a peer for fear of ridicule. However, if she can use the excuse, "My parents won't let me," this takes her off the hook and reduces, although not always, the likelihood of ridicule. The following is a common example of this type of thing: Katie receives a call on the telephone. Someone is asking her to do something she doesn't want to do. Within sight of her mother, and so that the caller can hear her, she yells out to her mother, "Mom, can I go to the beach with Katherine and her cousins tonight?" While she is asking her mother this, she is simultaneously shaking her head from side to side, signaling that she wants her mother to say no. Her mother gets the cue and says no. The friend on the other end of the line hears Katie's mother say no, and the conversation quickly comes to an end.

## NOT TAKING BEHAVIOR PERSONALLY

Probably one of the most significant things you can do to cope successfully with negative early adolescent behavior is not to take it personally. This point has been made over and over again for good reason. Taking early adolescent behavior personally can take a huge toll on your mental and emotional health and well-being. Once you understand what behaviors to expect of your child, as well as *why* he is behaving in a certain way, you should recognize and accept that these behaviors are normal. Every person must go through this developmental stage as you did once yourself. Try to remove your emotions from the situation and deal with things as objectively as possible. Understand that if your child rebels, is mouthy, or disassociates himself from you, he is being normal and is doing the things he is supposed to do in order to fulfill his developmental needs. The child is not behaving in that manner because you have done something wrong, because you are a bad parent, or because something is wrong with you. Of course, recognizing that this behavior is normal does not mean that you can't do something about controlling it and keeping it in check. At times during early adolescence, it will appear that your child doesn't love you or want you anymore. This is simply not the case. As unlikely as it may seem, it is important for early adolescents to be sure of their parents' love for them and for parents to be there when their children need them. Try not to let anything, such as your hurt feelings stand in the way of fulfilling this need for them.

## REMAINING CALM

Another thing you can do to make things easier during your child's early adolescent years is to try to remain calm. It is very easy to become impatient, frustrated, and stressed out with fear and worry during these years. Deal with the behavior as you must, but try not to "let it get to you." This is easier said than done, but if you can do it at least part of the time, it will reduce your stress load significantly. Understand what is normal with early adolescents, and try to accept it. By accepting the everyday moods, hates, loves, challenges, and annoyances as normal, you are less likely to lose your cool. You do not have control over the process of puberty. Your child is going to experience it whether you like it or not and whether you get "worked up" about it or not. Puberty is a normal part of human evolution, and fortunately for you, it doesn't last forever.

## DISCIPLINE

As a child progresses in age and development during early adolescence, disciplinary problems tend to increase, and parents must be prepared to deal with them. Developing good behavior management skills is important. Although parents should be understanding and sympathetic to early adolescents, and should support them through all of the changes they are experiencing, they must, at the same time, be firm in handling them. As a result of early adolescent development, parents are faced with behaviors they haven't had to deal with before, many of them difficult (such as rebellion and defiance). If good behavior management has been part of the relationship between you and your child from a young age, behavior during early adolescence will be more of a challenge to manage but will probably be kept under control. If discipline has been lax during the childhood years and the child is used to getting his own way with things, there will likely be problems in controlling and managing the child's behavior during the early adolescent years. However, if this has been the case, it is not too late to develop behavior management techniques; this should be done as early as possible in puberty. Stating your expectations and standards and developing rules that you consistently enforce are important practices.

One of the biggest mistakes parents of children (of all ages) make today is raising children who are undisciplined or minimally disciplined. When these children get to school and out into the world, they often have problems because they are used to having things their own way and doing as they please. This, of course, is not possible in a classroom of 30 children, and the school and other social agencies must then take on the responsibility of teaching the child to control his behavior. This is not always easy after the child has had his way for years. If the child's behavior is not corrected at some time during the school years, he may have problems dealing with authority when he is an adult. He may also have trouble accepting responsibilities and limits in society in general. If minimal or nonexistent discipline does not do the child any good, why do parents allow it to happen?

## WHY SOME PARENTS AVOID DISCIPLINE

First, some parents say they don't discipline their children because they love their child so much that they don't want to hurt him or not give him what he wants. Other parents feel that the child won't like them or will think they are "mean" if they discipline them. In families with two parents working outside the home, there is often a minimum amount of time to spend with their children, and many of these parents say they don't want to spend the time they have being negative, saying "no," or disciplining the child. This is also true of many single parents who have full responsibility for the care of their child while working full time and juggling other roles (such as housekeeping or meal preparation). They often feel guilty about not having enough time to spend with a child and may be permissive or give in to him to make him "happy" or to avoid being "disliked" by the child. The idea that children won't like parents if they punish or discipline them is a great fallacy among today's parents—nothing could be further from the truth. Children expect to be punished when they do something wrong. It rids them of the guilt they feel when they have done something they know is wrong. It also builds character and self-discipline and prepares children to deal with authority in society outside the home. Children need and want some structure, rules, and limits. Structure provides them with a sense of security, especially in today's changing world. When parents develop standards and rules and enforce them consistently, they not only restrict the child's behavior but also protect the child. Rules ensure a child's physical (safety) and emotional well-being. Without them, a child feels very insecure and unable to do anything about it. A rule, then, is both a constraint and a guarantee of emotional freedom. The child knows that if something is bad for her, her parents will not allow it. Children know where they stand. Expectations are clear, and the child develops a set of values and standards and a sense of right and wrong. Setting limits also helps to prepare children for adult life where they won't always be able to do what they want because there are rules and limits.

If parents discipline their children, this doesn't mean they don't love their children. They love their children, hug them, show them affection, and praise them for their good behavior. The children, in return, love and respect their parents, even though their parents sometimes discipline them.

Another reason parents don't discipline children is because they think that if they ignore the behavior or problem, it will go away. Or the parents may feel that it is too difficult, troublesome, or inconvenient to discipline the child. It is easier just to overlook the problem. If a child's behavior is not kept under control and he is allowed to do as he pleases, it won't belong before the child will take control of the parents or family. As hard as it may be to believe, a growing number of parents are seeing child psychologists because their 5- or 6-year old child's behavior is so out of control that the child runs the parents rather than the parents running the child. Imagine what the situation will be like when those children reach early adolescence, when disciplinary problems come to a peak! Behaviors must be corrected when inappropriate and controlled when deviations occur. Otherwise, how will children learn? How will they know right from wrong? How will they feel secure?

During early adolescence, lax discipline can very quickly lead to major problems. Inappropriate behavior cannot be ignored but must be dealt with because it can quickly escalate out of control.

## DEVELOPING EFFECTIVE
## BEHAVIOR MANAGEMENT TECHNIQUES

In developing behavior management techniques for early adolescent children, the following are some points to consider:

1. In setting up rules and guidelines for your child to follow, think them through carefully, in advance whenever possible. Consider all possible alternatives, and choose the one that best suits the child's needs and your own beliefs and standards. Although it is not possible to do this all the time, most of your decisions will be sound and enforceable if you practice this rule.

This is because you have given the rules considerable thought rather than making decisions on the spur of the moment, which you may regret later on. Try to anticipate in advance any major rules you know will have to be made. An example might be when your child will be allowed to date. If your daughter is on the phone one day and asks if she can go out with Matthew, the conditions are less than ideal for making an important decision such as this one. If you make a decision about this in advance and let your child know that she cannot date until she is 15 or 16, the child will proceed on that basis. (This does not mean that she won't try to get you to change your mind in the meantime.)

2. When it is appropriate, involve your child in establishing and setting the rules she will have to follow (for example, when she will clean her room and what penalty she will face if she does not follow through). This gives the child a sense of ownership and increases the possibility that she will adhere to the rules. If you feel it would be helpful, write out the rules (or have her do it), and post them as a reminder or for reference.

3. Once established, rules and penalties should be consistently applied and enforced. Relenting on any rule will send the child the wrong message. The child will think that you don't really mean what you say because when he breaks a rule, he is not punished or is only sometimes punished. Thus, the child will be willing to take a chance on breaking a rule because there is a good possibility that he will get away with it. You can't expect consistent behavior from a child if enforcement is not consistent. An example: David comes home past his curfew. Sometimes he is punished, while other times he is not. On this basis, he is willing to take a chance that he won't be punished "this time" and will continue to violate the curfew.

4. When rules and guidelines have been established, expect your child to test them. This is a normal activity of early adolescents.The way in which these initial confrontations are handled will have a significant effect on future behavior. If the child sees you are sticking to the enforcement of the rule, he will not likely

engage in the behavior too many more times afterward. However, if he gets away with it, he will continue to test you in the future, setting a permanent pattern.

5.  Keep rules to a reasonable, workable number for serious or more important things. If there are too many rules governing every little thing, the child will feel very boxed in and frustrated. Early adolescents need some breathing room. Let them have it in matters that are not important. Many of the small things can be overlooked. Early adolescents need to feel that they are getting away with something. If they do this with small matters, it is not a big deal. Keep the rules for more significant things.

6.  Think through appropriate punishment for the child when she does not abide by a rule. Make the punishment fit the crime. Try to do this when you are in a calm frame of mind or when you have "cooled off." The punishment should be fair and suit the seriousness of the behavior. Generally, consequences for breaking rules should follow as soon as possible afterward.

7.  Make sure the punishment is fair, realistic, and enforceable. For example, a parent in a fit of rage tells her child that he is "grounded" for six months. This is very severe and will be difficult to enforce. It is also not very realistic. Six months is a very long time to an early adolescent. Usually what happens in these cases is that the parent eventually has to relent and make the time span smaller and smaller. If this is done repeatedly, the child is no longer deterred because when he hears that he is grounded for six months, he knows it will be only a week or two.

8.  Avoid making threats that you cannot carry out. This usually happens when you are in a state of anger or frustration. When you threaten to do something and then don't follow through, any future threats you make will not be taken seriously by the child because he will get the message that you are all talk and no action. If you threaten, be prepared to follow up. For example, don't say to your son, "If your room is not cleaned, you are not going to the baseball game with us" and then let the child go without having cleaned his room.

9. Think through the introduction of new freedoms, privileges, or behaviors (such as staying out later). Once you allow a child to stay out later or go out on a date once or twice, it will be very difficult to revert back to the previous situation and disallow it. "Just this once" is rarely that.

10. Be skeptical of your child's reports that everyone else has something or everyone else is allowed to do something. Early adolescents have a tendency to think that other kids have more privileges than they actually do. Just because other kids can do something is no justification for you to allow it for your child if you feel it is not right. One or two kids in a class may say that they are allowed to do something, and the rest of the children in the class hear of it, whether it is true or not. They go home and lobby their parents to let them do it because "everyone else is doing it." By the time each child lobbies his or her own parents, the percentage of kids who can do it will probably increase because each parent thinks that if everyone else is doing it, maybe he should allow his child to do it too.

If discipline has been lax in the past, it is not too late to start over again. The initial period will be difficult because the child is used to different standards. However, once you show that you are consistent in your behavior management, he will get the message.

## RECOGNIZING POSITIVE BEHAVIOR

Of course, we must not forget that positive behavior in early adolescents should be recognized and praised. Reward early adolescents by telling them how well they are doing. Encourage them to continue with positive behaviors, and be supportive of any positive endeavors they undertake. Early adolescents need encouragement and constant support during this period of insecurity. They need to know that you love them, that you are proud of them, and that they can always come to you for help or support when they need it. Praise them as often as circumstances warrant. It is so easy to forget about the positive aspects of early adolescent behavior during difficult times.

## EARLY ADOLESCENTS' UNWILLINGNESS TO LISTEN

One of the most common complaints parents have about early adolescents is that they don't listen. While this point has been discussed in many respects previously, there is another important aspect of it that parents should be aware of. Most early adolescents do not seem to learn from other people's experiences and mistakes. Adults often feel that by offering advice based on their own experiences, they can help early adolescents avoid mistakes and pitfalls. But early adolescents want to cut loose from established authority and figure things out for themselves. Thus, advice from adults is not always heeded or accepted. Early adolescents usually learn things the hard way. They have to learn by experience, through trial and error, and by making mistakes. No amount of information or experience adults provide for them will entirely eliminate the need for them to discover and experience things on their own.

One of the most difficult things for parents to do is to stand by and watch their child make mistakes. Nonetheless, when making mistakes does not involve any long-term harmful effects to the child, early adolescents should be allowed the experience of making mistakes. While you may guide and direct your child, offer input and advice, or discuss the situation with the child, it is not good to deny them the experience of making mistakes. It is also not good to structure the environment in a manner where a child cannot make mistakes and is prevented from the negative consequences of doing so. Although early adolescents aren't very realistic about things at times, they have to learn to live in the real world. Not allowing early adolescents to make mistakes and learn from their mistakes only postpones the inevitable. It will make it harder for the child to learn to accept failure and to learn to stand on his own two feet someday.

If you recognize that your child is making a bad decision, talk to her about it. Explain your perspective of things. If she makes the wrong decision, she will suffer the consequences and will, in retrospect, realize her mistake. Without admitting it to you, she will also recognize the fact that you were right. Allowing early adolescents to make mistakes is difficult to do, but it is a necessary step on the road to independence. If, however, you feel your child is making a decision or mistake that is serious or will cause her harm or put her in jeopardy, that is the time to step in and use your authority to prevent such a thing from happening by not allowing her to proceed with the action or decision.

## RESPONSIBILITY

As they grow older, early adolescents should be given more and more responsibility. This can include being responsible for doing things around the house (for example, doing dishes, taking out the garbage) or doing things outside of the home (for example, babysitting). Accordingly, early adolescents can be given some privileges and freedoms (such as staying out later) when they are responsible enough to handle them. If they cannot handle their privileges and new freedoms responsibly, the privileges should be taken away and reintroduced at a later time. Each child differs in his or her ability to handle freedoms and responsibility. Some children are more mature than others and therefore better able to handle privileges at an earlier age.

While early adolescents want to have new freedoms and privileges, they also want the security of not having to accept responsibility for the consequences of their actions if they "mess up." But early adolescents must learn to accept responsibility for their actions. They can no longer assume that their behavior will be dismissed by others on the premise that "he is only a child."

When talking about accepting responsibility, tell your child that all people have responsibilities once they are no longer children. It is part of growing up. If people do not fulfill their responsibilities, it causes other people problems. For example, ask him how he would like it if you "forgot" to do his laundry one week or didn't make dinner every night because you didn't feel like it. What if you didn't go to work because you didn't feel like it and then you couldn't pay your bills, buy food, and so forth. Use these types of examples as well as others you can think of from society at large to illustrate this point.

## TALKS AND DISCUSSIONS

Talking things out and discussing problems with early adolescent children is important and usually beneficial even though it may not appear that any good has been done. Clear communication with early adolescent children reduces the number of misunderstandings and leads to fewer problems. When in doubt about how your child is feeling, talk to him about it. If you want your child to know how you are feeling, tell him about it.

Getting a message through to your child by way of "speeches" and "lectures" can also be beneficial at times, if it is not overdone. Even though these messages are usually given at a time when you may be upset, the message will usually get through—if not immediately, then later. It is important for you to recognize that your talks, discussions, and occasional lectures are effective, whether it appears that they are or not. You are not wasting your time. In the long run, the results will be worthwhile.

## WAYS TO MAKE COMMUNICATION
## MORE EFFECTIVE

When you talk to your child, there are several things you can do to make the communication more effective:

1. First, be sincere. This age group values sincerity and authenticity. Early adolescents are beginning to see through people, and if you are being less than honest, they will probably detect it. Furthermore, they will be insulted that you think they are "stupid" or "a baby" because you think you can fool them. As a result, they will likely accuse you of thinking they are not very intelligent, and they will be reluctant to discuss things with you in the future.

2. If the child wants to talk about something, many times what she really wants is someone to listen to her. On these occasions, listen to the child and let her finish her story without offering advice (unless it is asked for). Talking about a problem often provides the child with a way to relieve frustration. At these times, listening to the child is very important. Resist the temptation to butt in and take over the conversation. Check for understanding by rephrasing the child's comments in your own words and repeating them back.

3. Don't belittle the child's problem or conversation. A matter that you may consider trivial or of little importance may be important to him. Try not to make his concerns look trivial next to your adult problems.

4. Try not to be too critical when your child is talking to you. This takes tremendous willpower, but if a child thinks that all he is going to get from talking to you is criticism, he's not likely to approach you again. Unsolicited advice is often perceived as criticism.

5. When discussing how you feel about something with a child, try to use statements that describe how the child's behavior makes you feel ("I" statements) rather that using blaming statements directed at the child ("you" statements). For example, "*I* get angry when . . . (you are late for dinner) because . . . (*I* have to keep your food warm until you arrive) and then . . . (*I* can't finish cleaning up the dishes or supper table, which means I end up doing these jobs twice). This way of communicating the message is preferable to, for example, "*You* make me mad when you're late for dinner. *You* have no consideration for me."

6. Finally, don't say "I told you so." You can think it a hundred times, but don't say it. Early adolescents hate to hear that line. They will realize that they were wrong about something and you were right. They will be frustrated as a result. They don't want to have it "shoved down their throats," as the saying goes.

## TEACHING EARLY ADOLESCENTS TO FACE PROBLEMS

While talking things out with early adolescents is important, teaching them to deal with their problems is equally important. Early adolescents need to learn that everyone has problems and that problems must be faced and dealt when they arise. They need to know that running away from a problem doesn't solve anything and isn't going to make the problem go away. Unfortunately, many runaways and those involved with alcohol and drugs use these to escape from their problems. Of course, in doing so, they create even bigger problems. Point out that there are solutions to most problems even though the solution may not be exactly what they were hoping for. Tell the child that although she would like things to be a certain way, no one gets what he or she wants all the time, and it is unrealistic to think in these terms. Compromise solutions are needed at times. By teaching children to face problems and deal with them, eventually they learn to do so on their own. As a result, they may be less likely to become depressed or to seek drugs and alcohol as escapes or solutions to their problems.

When helping your child deal with a specific problem, ask him to first identify the problem and then think about what can be done to solve it. Ask him to suggest some ways to accomplish what he wants to happen. Suggest possible approaches to solving the problem, and without doing the thinking for him, help the child go through the problem-solving process. Steer and guide him through the process, but avoid the tendency to give advice during the session, unless you are asked for it.

## PRIVACY

As children grow older, they develop a greater need for privacy. The issue of privacy is very important to early adolescents, and some become obsessed with it. They feel they need to hide their body parts, hide new items of clothing (such as bras), and hide hygiene products (for example, deodorant or sanitary napkins). Much of this need for privacy stems from their insecurity and the awkwardness they feel as developmental changes occur. Hiding or keeping these things out of sight seems to lessen the embarrassment. It doesn't occur to early adolescents that they need not be embarrassed, because others use deodorant, wear bras, and so forth. However, because these things are new to them, early adolescents need time to adjust.

Privacy is also important to early adolescents in that it is another healthy and normal way to show early adolescents that they have become individuals of their own and that they are separating from their parents. Early adolescent privacy should be respected as it relates to their everyday lives. They need to have a private place to keep personal belongings, to change clothes, to bathe, and so on. Knocking on the bedroom door before you enter the room and other similar gestures are habits that should be cultivated. Avoid looking in their drawers or rummaging through their rooms without their consent. Don't read their diaries or personal notes. Begin to treat the child as you would another adult in matters concerning privacy. If you need to clean in your child's room, tell her ahead of time that you will be doing so, even if it's only five minutes ahead of time. That way she can remove anything from your sight she doesn't want you to see (for example, her diary, notes from friends). More often than not, the things that early adolescents are so concerned about keeping private are really no big deal to adults. They are not really anything adults would be interested in or concerned about. However, at times, when there are well-founded suspicions that the child's room may contain stolen property, drugs, alcohol, or evidence of serious deviant behavior, it is your duty and right to break the privacy rule for the good of the child.

## CRITICISM OF YOUR PARENTING ABILITY

Parents of early adolescents often feel uneasy when other adults, usually relatives, neighbors, or friends, continually criticize their child's behavior or their parenting techniques. It is easy for people to make such criticisms if they have not gone through the same parenting process themselves under the stresses of today's society. Do your best and try to ignore the outside input if it is not relevant or useful to you. Your child's and your family's best interests should be foremost in your mind and not what the neighbors think. They are going to think what they think anyway, so there is nothing to be gained in worrying about it.

In "secure" families, most parents, brothers, and sisters of early adolescents can learn to live with the problems of early adolescence until the period is over. Arguing and squabbles will persist but are normal. Research indicates that if parents had positive ties between themselves and their children before early adolescence, they will likely continue afterward, even though the intervening period will prove annoying and somewhat difficult. In families where problems already exist, the onset of puberty in a child can contribute to further disintegration of family life. In such cases, it would be wise to seek professional help. Childhood personality problems and attitudes are important predictors of problematic behavior in youth.

Throughout their emotional evolution, early adolescents remain insecure. They need constant reassurance of their worth and abilities and continual support from adults in the face of constant change. Contrary to the appearance that early adolescents project—that they no longer need or want adults—they have a strong need for parental support. The entire world of the early adolescent is based on change, and that is difficult for them to deal with. For this reason, they need stability and security. A stable and secure homelife and family life, and a relationship with parents who are always there when they need them, bring a great deal of security and satisfaction to early adolescents, although they will seldom admit it. Because stability is so important in the home during early adolescence, it is best to postpone or avoid any major moves or changes in family life at this time. Research has shown that experiencing the effects of parental divorce or other family instability can be more detrimental to a child during early adolescence than at any other time before the adult years.

While most people are working hard at parenting their children, most early adolescents are oblivious to the woes of their parents. They are so wrapped up in themselves and their own world that they forget that parents work hard and have needs and feelings too. Most early adolescents don't have the slightest idea of what it is like to be a parent. They do not recognize the responsibilities that go with it (such as jobs, bills, and household chores). They need to be reminded about what you do from time to time, even though they are not likely to internalize it until they are older.

## SIGNIFICANT PROBLEMS

Finally, if early adolescents are having significant problems academically, socially, or emotionally, deal with them as they arise. If you cannot help or solve a problem, or if you are having difficulty dealing with the child yourself for any reason, seek outside help. A school psychologist, guidance counselor, or school social worker can be of assistance. They are available through most schools. Getting help from a psychologist, psychiatrist, or social worker in private practice who specializes in working with children and adolescents can also be of benefit. Do not wait until the behavior or problems have gone to an extreme or until you no longer have control of the child before you seek help. The earlier the problem is recognized and intervention provided, the better the chances are of resolving it successfully.

# II

# TEACHING
# EARLY ADOLESCENT
# STUDENTS

# 10

# Teachers of Early Adolescent Students

Teachers have an important role to play in the lives and development of children. Aside from a child's parents and family members, teachers spend more time with children than anyone else. As a result, not only do they help them learn and grow academically, but they also serve as adult role models for children in both formal and informal settings, reflecting and representing the values held in common by society. In this respect, teachers can be a positive influence in the lives of children. This is particularly so with a growing number of children today who come from unstable homes and disintegrating families and who experience the ravages of child abuse, family violence, and many other problems. For some students, the teacher is viewed more positively and has more influence than the child's own parent(s).

Early adolescents need stable, consistent, and reliable adult role models who will guide them through the physical, social, emotional, and intellectual changes they experience as they become young adults. Because of the emphasis on social and emotional (affective domain) development during the middle school years, the middle school teacher serves as an adult role model for a broad range of student needs. Teachers of early adolescents serve not only as sources of academic development, but also as providers of guidance, models of social skill development, enhancers of self-esteem and personal growth, and so on. Middle-level teachers who are caring and understanding can have a very positive and sometimes major influence on the lives of their students.

Teaching early adolescent students is not always an easy job, however. The middle level, more than any other, has students who exhibit the greatest variety in terms of stages of intellectual, physical, social, and emotional development. Early adolescent behavior is very unpredictable. *Rebellious, defiant, moody, inconsiderate, smart-mouthed,* and *know-it-all* are just a few of the behavioral descriptors attributed to these students. Thus, teachers must be prepared for and committed to working with early adolescents. Those who are not prepared are potential candidates for unnecessary stress, frustration, burnout, and failure.

Early adolescents are rebelling against adults and adult authority. Just as parents are faced with negative behaviors that arise from early adolescent change and development, so are teachers. As adults and authority figures, they are not exempt. For parents, early adolescence is a phase of development in a child's life that is temporary and will eventually come to an end. This, however, does not happen for teachers of early adolescents. Each year they face a new group of students who will be experiencing puberty under their tutelage. Therefore, they must understand the characteristics and needs of early adolescents and must be prepared to deal with their behavior day after day, month after month, and year after year. For middle school teachers, there is no end to puberty.

Experienced teachers who have taught at various educational levels (grade school, middle school, and high school), consistently point to the middle school level as being the most challenging. Middle-level teachers experience more stress, burnout, and job dissatisfaction than those at other teaching levels. Much of the difficulty encountered by these teachers stems from an inability to manage the behavior of early adolescent children.

However, in spite of the difficulties they face, there are many successful middle-level teachers. These are teachers who would not choose to teach at any other level. They are individuals who enjoy working with early adolescents and who enjoy the satisfaction and rewards of guiding them through the transitional process of puberty and the traumatic ordeals it brings. They feel that by teaching at the middle level, they can really make a difference in the lives of their students, and they take great pride in their ability to do so. They find their teaching experiences with early adolescents unique, challenging, and rewarding. They are committed to the early adolescent student, and there is no other classroom where they would rather be. What makes these teachers successful? How do they avoid the distress and pitfalls that overcome others? What kind of person is best suited for teaching early adolescents?

## CHARACTERISTICS OF SUCCESSFUL TEACHERS

Like all teachers, middle-level teachers need to be qualified for their positions by having appropriate personality traits, a sound general education, and an interest in teaching and working with young people. The effective teacher of the middle level should certainly possess many of the traits of a successful teacher at other levels. But just as there are traits that lend themselves well to teachers of other teaching divisions (for example, kindergarten or high school), there are those that are more suited to middle-level teachers.

First, teachers who work at the middle level should genuinely like early adolescent children and have an interest and commitment to working with them. Much of a teacher's success in the middle school classroom is dependent on his or her ability to relate effectively to early adolescent students and establish a good working rapport with them. That means being able to understand early adolescents and their behaviors and being able to accept early adolescent students for what they are: children in transition who are confused, unsure of themselves, and lacking in self-confidence and self-esteem. Successful teachers of early adolescent students recognize that most of the unpredictable and negative behavior of early adolescents is normal and is related to their development. The negative behaviors of early adolescents seldom have anything to do with the teacher, what she has done, or what she is teaching, as students so often imply.

To work well with early adolescents, teachers not only must like early adolescents but must be knowledgeable about the nature, development, unique characteristics, and special needs of early adolescent children. They must understand the change processes that early adolescents experience in all areas of human growth and development, including the physical, biological, social, and emotional domains. They must understand the link between developmental change and typical early adolescent behavior. They must know how to channel early adolescent energies and how to motivate them. In other words, in order to respond to children's behaviors appropriately and to provide the best possible learning environment, teachers of early adolescent children must know what makes them "tick." Successful middle-level teachers understand their students, view them realistically, and have realistic expectations of them.

The middle school teacher must have a clear understanding of her value system and a strong self-concept and constitution. Like parents, teachers are a daily target of student frustration, anger, and moodiness. Early adolescents habitually take out their frustrations and anger on teachers who have nothing to do with the actual cause of their anger. For example, Benjamin tells a teacher that the topic for an art lesson is stupid and boring when he may really be venting his anger because a fellow student just made fun of his new shoes. The middle-level teacher must feel secure and be confident enough not to be bothered by such behavior. The middle-level teacher must be able to recognize this type of behavior for what it is and should not take negative remarks and criticism from the students personally because they usually have no validity. Teachers unfamiliar with early adolescent traits and development often do take this behavior personally and can become bitter and resentful of the students because they feel they are wasting their time with these "bad" students. It takes an especially resilient and tolerant person to work with such an unpredictable age group.

Middle-level teachers must also have personality traits that enable them to provide a consistent, secure working environment for early adolescent students. At a time when everything about them is changing, early adolescents need a secure classroom environment—one in which the teacher has control of himself as well as control of students at all times. Teachers who can provide this while maintaining a relaxed, warm, and friendly classroom atmosphere will gain the respect and cooperation of students. Early adolescents seem to lose respect for adults who can no longer control them. Their newfound ability to identify weaknesses in adults leads them to experiment and prey on those weaknesses simply to see the kind of reaction they can get. They also habitually test the confines of the adult world and adult authority. Teachers who remain calm, collected, and emotionally in control of themselves during these situations do well working with these children. Teachers who work well with early adolescent children are people who are usually relaxed and not overly excitable.

Middle-level teachers must also be very understanding of early adolescent problems. These children undergo a great transition within a relatively short period of time. It is a difficult process, during which they are often confused and frustrated and don't know where to turn or how to act. The teacher must be able to respond to their problems and needs in a caring and concerned manner. The ability to put oneself into a child's shoes from time to time and to remember what it was like to deal with all of these problems can be very helpful.

But while teachers must be sympathetic to early adolescents and their problems, they must also be firm in handling them. Classroom management skills are a necessary strength of middle-level teachers. Teachers of early adolescent students must be alert individuals in order to anticipate the types of discipline problems likely to occur in their classrooms. They must also have plans to deal with the problems effectively when they do occur. The inability to develop successful and effective classroom management techniques and disciplinary procedures is the prime cause of teacher dropout at the middle level.

Because early adolescent students are so unpredictable, flexibility is an important trait for teachers of these students. Plans, lessons, and routines are often disrupted or not completed in the intended manner during the course of a day or week. While teachers must always be prepared for each class they teach, they should not be too rigid in their adherence to plans when unexpected events occur or routines are disrupted. Many times, planned subject matter needs to be set aside in order to address real-life issues that arise and need to be dealt with. The teacher must be flexible enough to do the right thing at the right time. The unpredictability of the age group also means that teachers of this level must be able to think on their feet and to make decisions on a moment-by-moment basis when situations warrant.

Teachers of early adolescents must be people who enjoy a challenge. Many teachers of this level indicate that one of the things they like best about teaching early adolescents is working in an environment where there is never a dull moment. That is certainly an appropriate way to describe a middle-level classroom!

A sense of humor is also a very desirable trait of middle-level teachers, not only to help themselves cope but to provide some relief from the tension and anxiety that are common in middle-level classrooms. Occasional laughter, especially at oneself or one's predicament, can save many a lesson or day. An outrageous and humorous comment at the appropriate time can also diffuse a potentially explosive situation (such as student anger or frustration). Early adolescent students enjoy, appreciate, and respond warmly to humor when it is used appropriately. Of course, teachers should *never* make fun of or laugh directly at a student in a personal way. Such remarks can be devastating for students with fragile self-concepts or low self-esteem. Inappropriate humor can also result in the student developing a tremendous resentment toward the teacher or a desire to "get even." This often leads to an increase in behavioral problems.

Enthusiasm is another desirable quality of middle-level teachers. Early adolescents are not easy to motivate. Academics are not usually a priority in lives that are full of developmental change. Being enthusiastic, innovative, and creative in one's teaching approach and attitude is a definite plus. Teachers who tend to be extroverted may also find this to be an advantageous trait at this level. The ability to dramatize things (for example, reading literature in a theatrical manner) and the ability to be a bit of a showman at appropriate times (for example, getting dressed up as Santa Claus on the last day of school before Christmas) adds interest and vitality. Such an approach can provide motivation to students who would otherwise find subject matter dry and boring.

Teachers of early adolescents should be knowledgeable about the particular methodologies and classroom teaching skills that work best with early adolescents. They must be able to establish a classroom climate and atmosphere that suits the characteristics and needs of early adolescent students. Ways of doing this will be examined later.

In various surveys that have been done to determine what qualities middle-level students like or want in a teacher, the same traits tend to appear over and over again. These include the following characteristics: is helpful, friendly, honest, nice, fair, caring, patient, and kind; has a good sense of humor; is understanding; makes learning fun and interesting; listens to you; helps you with your problems; is in control of the class; likes kids; is smart; and knows how to teach. There are many parallels between these traits identified by middle-level students and those we have discussed thus far.

## MIDDLE-LEVEL TEACHER TRAINING

The best way to prepare oneself for teaching at the middle level is to be educated about early adolescent children and trained with the most effective methods of working with them. Such education and training are available in a growing number of teachers' colleges around the nation.

Over the past decade or two, as the middle school movement has continued to grow, many teacher training institutes have established specific courses, programs, and certification for those who teach at the middle level. More than 50 percent of states have now adopted some form of middle-level teacher certification. There is also a substantial movement toward the requirement of both middle-level teacher preparation and separate middle school certification in order to teach at the middle level. While no program can prepare a student teacher completely for the reality of a school classroom, effective teacher education programs can make a significant difference in the comfort level and effectiveness a teacher experiences once he begins to teach. Student teachers who are educated with a solid base of information about middle-level teaching and early adolescent development seldom suffer from the levels of anxiety, stress, and frustration experienced by teachers who have not had the benefit of this training. Education also significantly reduces the amount of time needed for new teachers to become comfortable and effective at middle-level teaching. This contrasts with teachers who have no specific education on middle-level teaching and who must learn about it on their own by trial and error and through experience over an extended period of time.

## STRUCTURING THE MIDDLE SCHOOL CLASSROOM

An important part of the middle-level teacher's job is establishing an optimal learning environment that provides the physical and psychological components necessary for student growth and development.

From a psychological point of view, the middle-level classroom should be a warm and friendly place where students feel physically and psychologically safe within the context of the school and society at large. Stability and security are essential. Early adolescents want to be in a classroom where the teacher is in control. It is difficult for a young person whose whole world is changing to cope with all of the changes. Providing a reasonably structured and secure classroom without stifling creativity and inciting unnecessary fear adds stability and security. Students need to feel a sense of belongingness in the classroom; they need to feel accepted regardless of their backgrounds or differences. Early adolescents want to be treated fairly and with dignity and respect. They need to feel free to ask questions, make comments, and volunteer answers without fear of ridicule, putdown, or rejection. A warm and inviting classroom inspires a sense of pride in the students who work within it.

The physical environment is an important part of an effective classroom environment. Each teacher has the responsibility of arranging the physical elements of the classroom (such as desks or tables) to best support the learning environment and her teaching style. This will vary from teacher to teacher and from subject area to subject area. There are, however, some general principles that can help a teacher decide on an appropriate physical arrangement for the classroom.

First, it is necessary to ensure that the classroom has good ventilation, lighting, and temperature control. Students who are too cold or too hot cannot work efficiently, and they become restless. This is particularly so of early adolescents who have low tolerance levels and limited attention spans, are easily distracted, and cannot sit still for long periods of time. As they concentrate on the cause of their discomfort rather than the learning task at hand, they become disengaged from the learning process and can easily become disruptive, causing unnecessary problems and disturbances as a result.

The middle-level classroom, like other classrooms, should be neat and well organized. Not only is this visually appealing, but it is necessary for an efficient environment where everything has a place and where all students know they can find the things they need at any given time.

An important consideration regarding furniture in the middle-level classroom is the need to have a variety of different-sized desks available. This is necessary to accommodate the unusually great differences in physical size and development among early adolescent students. Two students who are the exact same chronological age can have significant differences in height and weight. Each student must be accommodated according to his or her level of physical development. For some students, changes will be needed several times over the course of the academic year.

Students should be seated in the classroom in such a way that all of them can clearly see the teacher and blackboard at all times. The teacher's desk should be strategically placed so that each student is within the teacher's sight, thus allowing all students to be monitored simultaneously. Traffic patterns in the classroom should provide for efficient movement around the room and should be developed in such a way that they do not entice students to misbehave. Students who are behaviorally problematic need to be seated where the teacher can monitor their behavior closely at all times. They should also be seated where they will not have an audience to misbehave for and where they cannot be easily distracted or disruptive of others (that is, they should be seated away from the pencil sharpener, waste basket, or other areas of student activity). Seating children who misbehave well away from others who are so inclined will also reduce the incidence of misbehavior in the long run. In summary, the physical learning environment should be structured for maximum teaching and learning efficiency and minimal disruption or nonproductive behavior.

As for learning materials and resources such as reference books, maps, dictionaries, and atlases, there needs to be a place for everything, and everything should be kept in its proper place. An orderly system is required to enable each student to remove and replace resources in an organized and efficient manner. That way, materials are easy to find when needed, and a determination can be made as to which student has a particular resource at any given time. Such organization also reduces confusion and lost instructional time. As always, the teacher is the role model for neatness and organization. Rules must be established regarding the use of classroom resources and the movement of students around the classroom.

Room appearance is important in providing an inviting atmosphere, a sense of warmth, and a sense of belonging. The room should appear colorful, interesting, and uncluttered. Displays of student work attractively arranged and bulletin boards related to current studies create motivation and encourage an active and inspirational learning atmosphere.

# 11

# Classroom Management

Good classroom management skills are a must for teachers of early adolescent students. In fact, effective classroom management skills can mean the difference between success and failure at the middle level. The prime cause of teacher dropout at the middle level is the inability to develop effective classroom management procedures.

In the process of rapid developmental change, early adolescents display many perplexing, difficult, and negative behaviors such as moodiness, rebelliousness, instability, and defiance. They can easily become unruly, and they frequently test adult authority, norms, rules, and values. Add to this their extreme restlessness, shortened attention spans, easy distractibility, fluctuating energy levels, and need to socialize and it becomes clear that managing the behavior of these students can be a challenge. In addition, teachers in middle schools today deal with misbehavior once considered problematic only to secondary-level teachers.

Discipline problems, more than any other factor, are the greatest cause of lost instructional time in the middle-level classroom. The more time teachers spend dealing with misbehavior, the less time there is left for teaching and learning. Since research strongly suggests a positive relationship between time spent "on task" in the classroom and student achievement, the goal of educators is to maximize learning time by minimizing disruptions and discipline problems. When an individual student misbehaves, he not only wastes time for himself, but also causes other students to be "off task" and disengaged from the learning process. Additionally, while the teacher is dealing with his behavior, she cannot teach or actively work with others in the class. Well-managed classrooms have minimal disruptions and fewer behavioral problems. Students spend as much time as possible on the task of learning.

Many of the behavior problems and disruptions that occur in middle-level classrooms stem from petty annoyances. Examples of this behavior include students calling each other names, grooming themselves (combing hair), chewing gum, talking to others, and passing notes. While each incident of this behavior is not considered serious in itself, when it is engaged in by a large number of students consistently over time, it can develop into a significant problem for teachers. Teachers then need to be continually dealing with these trivialities rather than engaged in the instructional process.

Another aspect of early adolescent behavior that can be frustrating to deal with is willful misbehavior, that is, students misbehaving on purpose just to see what kind of reaction they can get from the teacher. This type of behavior tends to anger teachers more than any other because it is perceived as a challenge to their rules and authority. It can also be taken as a personal affront: for example, "I just told him not to do that two minutes ago, and now he is doing it. Doesn't he think I mean what I say, or does he take me for a fool?" It must be recognized that this type of behavior is common among early adolescents. And while it should not be taken personally, the behavior must be dealt with effectively in order to keep it under control. Any weakness or inability of the teacher to control student misbehavior is likely to be tested over and over again by students. This can result in a loss of control in the classroom.

Other common problems teachers face in the middle-level classroom today are lack of student motivation, lack of student cooperation with regard to obeying classroom rules, student inattentiveness, extensive and inappropriate talking, student disobedience, disruptive behavior, and incomplete classroom assignments, homework, or projects.

## THE PREVENTIVE APPROACH TO CLASSROOM MANAGEMENT

Experts on the subject of classroom and behavioral management as well as experienced teachers of the middle level agree that the preventive approach to classroom management produces the best results at the middle level. The preventive approach focuses on anticipating problems and misbehavior in advance and preventing them from occurring rather than waiting for problems to occur and then reacting to them. For teachers, the preventive approach means doing all that is possible in the way of establishing a classroom atmosphere, developing classroom rules, and arranging the physical environment of the classroom to prevent problems and disruptions from occurring. Teachers using this approach structure the learning environment in such a way that students have few opportunities to misbehave or wander off task. When problems arise, they are dealt with as subtly as possible with minimal disruption to the rest of the class. The least disruptive method is the one that should always be chosen to deal with problems when they arise. Many problems in the classroom can be handled without disrupting student learning.

The preventive approach requires thorough planning of lessons and student activities. Students should always have something to do. Free time and idle students are an invitation for problems. Middle-level teachers must always be prepared for their classes. "Winging it," or making up a lesson as you go along without preplanning, is not a good idea at the middle level, and it seldom works. Any unplanned time that is not addressed during a class can lead to behavioral problems and student socializing.

As a motivational technique, some teachers develop a rule that if students are attentive and behave well during the class, they are rewarded by having the last five minutes of the class as free time. Of course, the teacher must then be prepared to monitor the students during the free time to ensure that the behavior and activity remain within acceptable limits. In any event, because of the unpredictable nature of the middle-level classroom, it is a good idea for teachers to have extra planned activities on hand or some sort of lesson or contingency plan that can be tucked away and then retrieved for use when needed.

Using the preventive approach, the middle-level teacher must be alert to any potential disruption and must intervene early to diffuse it or to prevent it from occurring. The teacher must continually anticipate possible problems that might occur in the classroom and must think of ways to avert them. When a potential problem is detected, it should be quickly headed off with an unobtrusive strategy. Once a teacher is familiar with his students on an individual basis, he is in a good position to anticipate behaviors. For example, Dennis is a student who is constantly seeking attention. To seat him in a desk at the front of the class with an audience readily available to him would be a big mistake. He is more likely to misbehave more often because he knows that everyone in the class can see him at all times, and he will likely take advantage of the fact to "clown around" and to act out in front of his peers. However, if he is seated at the back of the classroom or in a place where most students can't see him, it will be more difficult for him to misbehave. Since he has to attract an audience first, chances are that while he does that, the teacher is likely to intervene and prevent him from carrying out his intended disruptive behavior.

An awareness of and the ability to use a wide range of proven behavior management techniques is essential for middle-level teachers. Because of personality differences and variations in teaching styles among teachers, techniques that work well for some may not be used as successfully by others. Some techniques might also work well in some circumstances and not in others.

There are, however, some general techniques that have been used by a majority of successful middle-level teachers time and time again. We will now examine some of the most common successful strategies for classroom management at the middle level.While many of these techniques are not exclusive to the middle level of education, they work particularly well with early adolescent students.

## ESTABLISHING CLASSROOM RULES AND ROUTINES

Establishing sensible routines to be used in the classroom creates an organized and efficient classroom, saves time, and increases student learning. Clear routines in the classroom also help to eliminate confusion and unnecessary questions. When students are clearly aware of the procedures to be followed for any given activity, they are more likely to comply with them in an orderly and timely fashion. Routines and rules should be established for any common repetitive activity carried out in the classroom. Examples are when to sharpen pencils, procedures for visiting the restrooms, how assignments are to be handed in, and how students are to enter and leave the classroom.

A list of classroom rules needs to be developed, preferably at the beginning of the school year or semester. Soliciting student input in making rules will give them some ownership in the situation. Keep classroom rules simple, and keep them to a minimum number. Once the decisions concerning these rules have been established, they need to be clearly communicated to students. Discuss what is expected of them as well as the consequences of breaking rules. It is a good idea to post the rules somewhere in the classroom as a reminder to students. Word rules simply and state them in a positive way (for example, "Always walk in the classroom" rather than "Don't run around the classroom").

Parents might also be notified as to what is expected of the students. In many schools, a letter from the school is sent home to parents explaining school policy regarding student behavior. When this is not the case, a teacher might send home a notice of classroom policy outlining rules of student behavior. When this is done, the policy paper should be cleared with the school administration first to ensure that school administrators are in agreement with the teacher on the matters involved. That way, in the event of an infraction, the administrators are aware of a teacher's policies and in a position to support a teacher's actions.

Once rules and routines are established for the classroom, they should be consistently enforced. This is particularly important at the middle level because early adolescents have a strong sense of what is fair and what is not. Failure to enforce a rule is often interpreted by students as favoritism or weakness on the part of the teacher. Early adolescents are very concerned about things being done fairly.

In all likelihood, once rules and routines are established, students will make a point of testing them. The way in which the teacher handles the initial confrontations will have a significant effect on student behavior patterns for the rest of the term or year. If incidents are dealt with quickly and effectively, they will not likely occur too often in the future. If these initial "testing" behaviors are ignored, or poorly dealt with, the undesirable behavior will likely escalate and result in more problems in the future. Middle-level teachers should expect that rules will be tested once they are made. Therefore, a plan of action for dealing with behavior needs to be developed ahead of time so that teachers are prepared for it when it first occurs.

## CLASSROOM MANAGEMENT TIPS

There are many things a teacher can do to manage a classroom efficiently at the middle level. Some of them are as follows:

1. Learn students' names within the first few days or weeks (in the case of multiple classes) of school, and use their names to address them as frequently as possible. This makes students aware that you know who they are, and it strengthens the rapport you have with them. Students feel good when a teacher makes an effort to greet or recognize them by name.

2. Have high expectations of student behavior and performance. Whether they are expressed verbally or nonverbally, teacher expectations are recognized by students, and they do affect student performance and behavior. Make excellence a priority.

3. Make a point of giving clear instructions when teaching or assigning work to early adolescents. Before giving instructions, check that everyone is listening and paying attention (that is, make eye contact with students). Put instructions on the blackboard, an overhead projector, or an instruction sheet. Check for understanding. When instructions are clear, the students are more likely to settle down to work sooner. If instructions are unclear, they are more likely to ask the teacher questions, consult peers, or shuffle around looking for clarification or required materials.

4. Consistent enforcement of rules and good behavior is advocated, but minor incidents of bad behavior can be overlooked or ignored under certain circumstances. These circumstances include times when students are doing things or saying things that are not harmful and the teacher is out of their range of vision or hearing (or students *think* the teacher is out of range). The following is a common example: You have just scolded a student about something in the hallway. The student watches you as you leave, and as soon as he thinks you are out of hearing range he says, "I'm not going to do that. It's stupid. I hate that teacher." He does this in order to vent frustration, to save face, or to look "cool" in front of his friend. If you are far enough away from the student that he perceives you may not hear what he is saying, then just ignore it. If, however, it is obvious to you and other students that you can hear what he said, then it must be dealt with.

5. Use praise liberally with students. It provides encouragement, support, and reassurance to students struggling with change and development. Early adolescents are very insecure and unsure of themselves. They are trying out many new roles and behaviors. By praising and reinforcing their good behaviors, they will be encouraged to continue in that vein. Use praise to recognize effort and achievement. Praise students individually when appropriate, or praise the class as a whole. Praise improvements or even partial successes when appropriate. Praise students privately as often as possible, and praise them publicly when appropriate, but be aware that public praise can backfire at times. When too much praise is publicly directed toward one or two students, their peers may taunt and tease them or call them names like "teacher's pet." Care must be taken when giving public recognition to ensure that this does not happen. As teachers of early adolescent students, it is important to praise students for any deserving reason, not just academic achievement. Look for opportunities to praise students for athletic ability, artistic ability, citizenship, courtesy, musical talents, appearance (hairstyle, clothes), good behavior, attendance, and so on.

There are many ways to give recognition and praise. A smile is a good way to begin. Just smiling at a student at the right moment can tell a student that he is doing well or that you approve. Have award assemblies to reward achievement, effort, and citizenship. Have tangible rewards when appropriate (such as pizza, popcorn, or movie tickets). Contact a student's parent to indicate that the student is improving or doing well. Ask another teacher to provide you with information about a student that will generate an opportunity for you to praise the student. For example, "Todd, Mrs. St. Hill tells me you have quite a science project going in her class" or "Mr. Errol says your behavior in art class has really improved in the last few weeks. I'm very happy to hear that."

6. Restlessness is very common in middle-level classrooms. Because of rapid bone growth and muscle development, students cannot sit still for long periods of time. Short attention spans and

low concentration levels also add to the problem of restlessness. When students get restless, behavior problems can easily develop. Restlessness can manifest itself in many ways. Examples are fidgeting and nervous behavior (tapping fingers or feet) and students squirming or shifting frequently in their seats, grabbing things from others, poking others, and starting fights or arguments.

On recognizing that an individual or the whole class is getting restless, use a preventive approach to eliminate or reduce the incidence of the problem. If the whole class is getting restless, rather than wait for a behavioral incident to occur, provide a one-minute stretch break. Allow students to stand up and stretch for a minute and then get back to work. This releases pent-up energy, wakes up the sleeper, gets the daydreamer back on course, and temporarily gets rid of "ants in the pants." Often, individual students may get restless. A teacher recognizing this behavior can use an intervention strategy before any misbehavior occurs. For example, have the student hand out papers, take a book back to the library, or take a book back to another teacher. (Have an agreement with another teacher that if a student shows up with an unwanted book, the teacher will know it belongs to you and will return it to you sometime later in the day.) Have the student carry something or reach up and get something for you. Do something to change the pace and provide a brief break with minimal disruption. Good judgment must be used in choosing a suitable diversion for the child involved because these diversions can backfire if they are not appropriate. Also, when you ask the child to do the task, do so as quietly as possible so as not to disturb other students or cause them to become distracted. Think of appropriate diversions ahead of time, and keep a few in mind so that when a diversion is needed on the spur of the moment, you will be prepared.

7. Many disruptions occur at transitional points in the school day (for example, while changing classes) or at break points in a lesson (for example, when changing books or changing from one activity to another). Try to make the transitions as smooth and

problem-free as possible. When students enter the class, for example, it is wise for a teacher to begin as soon as possible afterward, saving discussion and questions from individual students until the end of the period. This reduces the amount of free time students have while waiting for the class to begin. During this time, they can become engrossed in conversations and socializing with friends, which is difficult to break up when it is time to begin the class.

Various techniques can be used to get students focused immediately when they enter the classroom. Some teachers put a trivia question on the blackboard for students to think about while other students are coming in. The answer can be given before the class begins. Students can take turns developing trivia questions, and these can be used instead of the teacher's questions. Other teachers use advance organizers and post a list of all the books and materials that will be needed during a class. That way, when students enter the class, they can begin to get focused and retrieve what they need immediately. This saves valuable time and gets them settled sooner. Telling students ahead of time which books and tasks will be required also helps to avoid interruptions later in class.

8. A sense of humor can be an effective tool in managing classroom behavior provided that good judgment is used. Sometimes an outrageous statement can diffuse a potentially explosive situation, or a humorous comment can prevent an embarrassing situation from getting worse. For example, a student trips and falls on his way out of the classroom. The student is embarrassed as the students in the class turn to look at him. The teacher might say something like, "Are you that tired Fred? I didn't think I was working you that hard in class!" Injecting some humor into subject matter when students appear bored or restless can also help. When a humorous incident or anecdote presents itself, use it to your advantage. Once again, *never* laugh at a student, make fun of him, or make him the object of jokes. This can be devastating for early adolescents. Laugh *with* a child, not *at* him.

9. Sometimes peer pressure can be used to a teacher's advantage to control student behavior. Approaching and enlisting the support of behaviorally difficult students to initiate special projects and to resolve discipline problems with others can sometimes help. In some circumstances or classes, teachers can use a reward system to control behavior through peer pressure. A game-like atmosphere is created whereby groups in the class compete for a prize at the end of the week or month. Another example: If the class as a whole meets certain expectations, students are rewarded at the end of a given period of time. Under these competitive circumstances, when a teacher makes a comment such as, "Jason, please don't lose additional points for your group," other students will probably glare at Jason, and he will likely stop his misbehavior. In these cases, the student changes his behavior because peers are pressuring him to change, and he conforms because he does not want the disapproval of his peers. The rewards provided at the conclusion of such sessions can include free time in class, in the library, or outdoors as well as tangible things such as pizza, ice cream, or movie tickets.

10. Avoid raising your voice or yelling at the students too frequently. When teachers yell all the time, it loses its effect. If a teacher raises his voice only when there is something serious, students will take notice and respond because they get the message that the teacher is upset and they had better pay attention.

11. Avoid making threats to students (usually in anger) that you don't intend to carry out. A threat made but not carried out will not deter any students next time. This is a common mistake made by beginning teachers. When a threat is made and carried out, the students will realize you mean what you say. Then the next time a threat is made, they are more likely to pay attention. For example, don't tell the class that if they don't settle down, they will not see a video and then let them see it anyway when they have not complied. When you make a threat, be sure it is something you are willing to carry out if students do not comply.

12. Although warmth and friendliness are desirable charac-

teristics of teachers of early adolescents, these teachers should avoid trying to be like early adolescents by acting like them or by becoming one of their "buddies." Early adolescent students are insecure and need firm role models. They want the important adults in their lives to act like adults and to be in control of themselves. This provides them with a sense of security and stability. Early adolescents want a teacher who is a friendly role model. They don't need another buddy or friend. They have plenty of those among their peers.

13. Finally, recognize that early adolescents learn from mistakes. While experimenting, trying out out new roles, and exerting their independence, they will make many mistakes. Expect them to do this. As adults, we feel that we can tell them what to do based on our experiences and knowledge, and that if they follow our advice, that will be enough. Unfortunately, it doesn't usually work that way. Early adolescents must experience things for themselves and learn things through experience and by trial and error. Do not take it personally when early adolescents choose to follow their own course of action rather than listen to your advice.

## MANAGING STUDENT BEHAVIOR (DISCIPLINE)

A variety of behavior management or discipline strategies can be used successfully with early adolescent students. While some strategies are effective with the majority of students most of the time, no one strategy works with all students all of the time in all situations. Therefore, a middle-level teacher should have knowledge of a wide repertoire of behavior management strategies in order to be prepared with plenty of options with which to deal with students every day. Some successful middle-level strategies that teachers can use to manage early adolescent behavior are as follows:

1. Be constantly alert to what is going on in the classroom (that is, what you see, hear, and sense). Scan the room frequently

or as often as possible, looking for potential problems. Students are less likely to misbehave if they know they are under constant observation.

2. Move around the classroom purposefully but on a random basis from time to time. It is a good practice to move about just after work has been assigned. This encourages students to begin work immediately and allows you to discreetly answer questions or clarify directions for those who need it without having to disturb others in the class.

3. When engaged in teaching or classroom discussion, monitor student attention and redirect it if it wanders. Do this subtly by simply looking at the student and catching his attention. When necessary, use verbal methods that do not involve singling the student out. For example, rather than say, "John, pay attention," say, "John, I want you to listen to Wilma's answer and tell me what you think about it."

4. It is a good practice to require periodic responses of all students in the class. This keeps them attentive. They are more likely to listen carefully if they think that they might be called on at any moment to give a response or provide input. If the same students are called on over and over again, or if only students who volunteer answers are called on, those who do not volunteer will eventually "tune out" and become inattentive. When posing a question, call on students who will not get into difficulty answering the question. This will build their confidence.

5. When a potential behavior problem has been identified, various techniques can be used to deter the undesired behavior and redirect the student's attention to the task at hand. For minor problems, the following techniques can be used:

(a) Use direct eye contact, such as looking at or glaring at a student, or use a stern facial expression. Just by looking at her, the student will know that you know what she is up to. As a result, she will most likely redirect herself back to the task at hand simply because you are watching her.

(b) Use a gesture to redirect or arrest behavior. For example, pointing to a student's desk if you notice she is wandering around will tell the student that you expect her to sit down.

(c) Look at or move in the direction of a disturbance (for example, two students passing notes). This will deter behavior because students know you are aware of what they are doing, and they do not want you to come over to talk to them about it or, in this case, confiscate the notes.

(d) Gently place your hand on a student's shoulder to redirect him to the task at hand. If the student knows you are right there watching, he is unlikely to continue his behavior or inattentiveness. This technique is often used when a teacher is observing a student from behind. The student is unaware that he is being observed until the teacher's hand is felt on his shoulder.

(e) If silent gestures are ineffective or inappropriate, calling the student's name aloud but in a soft voice can be effective.

(f) If none of the aforementioned techniques works, or if they are inappropriate, going over to the student's desk and speaking softly to him in a firm voice without calling the attention of others might work.

If these techniques are not successful in deterring or arresting behavior or are not appropriate, then another level of strategies can then be considered. These include the following:

(g) Give a verbal reprimand, but make it short and quick.

(h) Put a student's name on the blackboard (or in a notebook) as a way of warning that any further unacceptable behavior will meet with more serious consequences. The student should be aware of those consequences ahead of time as a result of rules for classroom behavior set out earlier (for example, name plus two check marks means staying after school).

(i) Move a student's desk to isolate her somewhere within the room (for example, move the student's desk close to the teacher's so that the student can be monitored more closely).

(j) Remove or deny classroom privileges to the student (that is, student is not allowed to get out of his seat without permission for the remainder of the day).

6. When a verbal reprimand becomes necessary, if it can wait, ask that the student stay after class. Then the problem can be dealt with one on one, in the absence of other students and without disrupting the other students. Do not confront a student in the classroom in front of his peers. Confrontation often gives the student what he wants (that is, to upset the teacher or to get attention for being a troublemaker). In reprimanding early adolescents, never back a student into a corner during a confrontation. The student will feel extremely embarrassed in front of his peers, and he will be left with no choice (in his eyes) but to defend himself by escalating the argument or problem with you in order to retain his reputation and look good in front of his peers. If a problem is dealt with one on one after school when no one else is around, the student will not have his peers to worry about or perform in front of. He is more likely to listen and be cooperative during the disciplinary process because his reputation is not at stake and he has no audience. If he has to stay after school, other students in the class will know he is in trouble and that he is being dealt with or punished, but they will not know what is said or done. Often students will ask the disciplined student what the teacher said or did. Student responses are not always truthful. For example, they say things like, "He didn't do anything" or "I told the teacher off." Again these students are trying to preserve their reputations, demonstrate their independence, and show their friends that adults aren't going to boss them around. Most students making the inquiry are usually skeptical about the validity of such comments but keep the skepticism to themselves.

7. Insofar as it is possible, you should be the one to deal with behavioral or disciplinary problems in the classroom. Avoid frequently sending students out of the class to be disciplined by others. Teachers who do this are undermining their authority to deal with the students. In the minds of the students, it can send the message that the teacher can't handle them. This is perceived

as a sign of weakness on the part of the teacher, and students then become eager to test and take advantage of these teachers.

If problems persist with certain individuals, as they will from time to time, then assistance from outside of the classroom should be considered. Sometimes other teachers can be asked for suggestions or help with management techniques that they use successfully, or they might be asked about how they handle the particular student.

A note or call to the child's parent can make the parent aware of the negative behavior or, if more appropriate, a parent conference can be arranged to discuss the problem. Contacting the parent and discussing the problem allows the parent to intervene with the child before the behavior becomes serious. Often agreements can be worked out with parents to keep the child's misbehavior under control. When a child is aware that the teacher and the parent are working together to improve his behavior, success is more likely than if the teacher is working on it herself. During a parent conference, describe the child's problem and the need for improvement to the parent. When the parent expresses feelings or opinions, listen attentively. Ask the parent for her suggestions, or ask her how she manages the child successfully at home. Ask for the parent's commitment to help work on the problem, and develop a mutual plan on which to act. Keep in touch with the parent over time to inform her of any progress or lack of it.

When a behavioral concern is more serious or approaching serious, it is always a good idea to document a student's behavior in a log or diary on a regular basis. Have the documentation available so that if a parent conference is arranged, you will be able to show evidence of the type of behavior, when it occurred, how often, and so on.

8.  When parental intervention is ineffective or when a lack of parental interest, control, or support is evident, then a teacher must resort to help from administrators in the building, usually the vice principal. When approaching the vice principal or principal about a problem student, the problem should be described as it pertains to the student and to the teacher in the classroom. The

vice principal can then be asked for advice or help in dealing with the problem. He might speak to the student about his behavior or arrange for an appropriate behavior modification strategy or program. This can involve such things as having the student placed in a time-out area of the school or having after-school detentions. When this level of management is not effective, then professional help needs to be sought through other school support personnel, particularly the school psychologist or social worker. In rare cases, the student can be suspended or expelled from the school, or may be sent to an alternative program out of the school.

9. In applying or using any classroom management or disciplinary strategy, always use the one that will be the most effective but least disruptive under the circumstances. For example, try to redirect a student's attention first with a glare or another silent technique. Do not call out the student's name aloud as a method of first choice. Other students who were engaged in learning tasks will become unnecessarily disengaged by looking up to see why Leo's name is being called out. Middle-level students are easily distracted, have short attention spans, and are restless. Once their attention is diverted because of an incident occurring elsewhere in the classroom, it can be time consuming to get them settled and back on task. If this happens several times over the course of a lesson, much valuable learning time is lost.

10. Be consistent in your expectations of students and in the application of classroom management measures and disciplinary actions. Apply the same rules and consequences to all students. Lack of consistency will result in students trying to get away with things more often. For example, if a student is inconsistently punished for a particular negative behavior, she will take a chance on misbehaving more often on the chance that she will get away with it "this time." Multiply this by many students in the class, and problems mount. Lack of consistency can also be interpreted as favoritism toward the students who are not dealt with when they break rules. Other students may become resentful as a result.

11. Closely related to consistency is fairness. Teachers must be fair (or at least appear fair) to students at all times. Fairness is

very important to early adolescents, and they become extremely frustrated when they feel that they are not being treated fairly or equally. This means all student regardless of background, beliefs, aptitudes, culture, and gender must be dealt with fairly. There will be times, however, when students will feel they have been treated unfairly because another student did not get the same punishment for what appeared to be the same offense. If a student should voice this concern, she should be told that the situation may appear the same, but in fact the circumstances were different. Although you do not need to explain what the differences were, the student is made aware that you knew differences were there and your treatment of the case was different for that reason.

12. Being warm and friendly with early adolescent students promotes good rapport, but teachers must nonetheless act with authority and control when warranted. When enforcing a disciplinary action, explain the reason for the action, whether the students appear to accept it or not (a statement only, not a long-winded and detailed explanation). Research indicates that rebellious and defiant behavior increases when strict authority is imposed on students without ever explaining or discussing reasons for it. On the other hand, teachers who allow students to do as they please, who ignore negative behavior because it is too troublesome or annoying to deal with, or who ignore negative behavior hoping it will go away on its own can easily lose control of the class. Despite the rebellious, defiant, and disrespectful manifestations of early adolescents toward adults, they actually feel a sense of satisfaction when disciplined for their negative behaviors. Of course, they will never admit this to adults.

13. Allowing students their dignity is also part of the disciplinary process. Regardless of what students have done, they are still human beings. While their behavior does not always show it, the early adolescent self-concept is fragile, and their sense of self-worth is low. During the disciplinary action, make it clear that the student's *behavior* is what is unacceptable and not the student himself. The student should understand that he is being reprimanded for what he has done and not for who he is. When

speaking to the student, make an effort to separate the person from the behavior.

14. Never embarrass students in front of their peers. This is interpreted by early adolescents as a fate worse than death. It can create extreme resentment toward a teacher as well as the desire to "get even." This only leads to more problems in the future. Similarly, teachers should never use sarcasm or ridicule a student.

15. When a student is disciplined, be sure that he clearly understands the reason. While it is usually evident, at times a student can be unsure. In some cases, because of cultural differences or the child's upbringing, the reason may not be clear to him. A good way to be sure that the student understands the reason for the disciplinary action is have him explain it or repeat it back to you. The student does not have to agree with the punishment but he needs to know why he is being punished. Students also need to know that they cannot violate certain rules and rights without penalty and that they do not have the right to disrupt the learning of other students.

When early adolescents are confronted about their misbehavior, it is common for them to immediately deny any wrongdoing. They also often fabricate elaborate and creative excuses for their behavior. Consider this a normal early adolescent response, and continue to deal with the problem as you normally would. If ever you do make a mistake in disciplining a student who does not deserve it, it is best to admit it and to apologize to the student as soon as possible. In the eyes of the students, this will generate more respect for you, your judgment, and your ability to be fair in the long run.

# 12

# Teaching and Intellectual Development

As discussed in Chapter 7, several generalizations can be made about the early adolescent intellect. We will now briefly review these characteristics and then examine the implications they have for teaching early adolescent students and developing and implementing the curriculum at the middle level.

## THE TRANSITION FROM CONCRETE TO ABSTRACT

The most significant characteristic of the early adolescent intellect is its changing nature. Early adolescents are in a transitional state between concrete and abstract thinking. When a child begins early adolescence, he does so as a concrete thinker. A child in the concrete thinking phase organizes information around categories or concepts that are visible and identifiable. The child needs concrete referents. He needs to see something in order to formulate opinions about it. Moving out of early adolescence, a child begins to think formally. The onset of formal thinking represents the beginning of adult thought processes. When formal thinking develops, children begin to think about and visualize things and possibilities without the need to see them. They begin to develop a sense of perspective and time. Before the age of 14, the majority of early adolescent students have not reached the stage of formal or abstract thinking, but they are able to experience this kind of thinking in its early stages or at a simple level. Between ages 14 and 16, however, formal thinking skills are established in the majority of students (where the capacity exists). These skills are then carried into adulthood where they are refined over time.

For middle-level teachers and those developing a curriculum for the early adolescent student, this transitional factor must be considered in the development of suitable learning materials. Curricula, lesson plans, learning activities, and skill development programs should focus on skills that suit the transitional nature of the early adolescent intellect. These include skills that bridge the gap from concrete to abstract and that guide and direct the child from concrete to abstract in a logical and sequential fashion.

Most early adolescent students operate in the concrete domain most of the time. As they begin to acquire and use skills of abstract thought (such as reasoning, hypothesizing, and analyzing), they are not consistent in the use of these skills. Each student develops these abilities at his or her own rate and time, and therefore great variations exist from child to child. A student can demonstrate formal reasoning at certain times or in a particular subject area, while operating in the concrete mode at other times and in other subject areas. A teacher cannot assume that a child has reached the level of formal thinking if he demonstrates this on only a few occasions or in one or two subject areas.

The transition from concrete to formal thinking is also not spontaneous. It needs guidance and direction from teachers. Whenever possible, lessons should begin with a concrete principle or concept and then move toward the simple abstract. This should be done in a logical, sequential, and stage-wise fashion.

Starting with a concrete base means beginning with what is familiar to the students before leading them to new interpretations or skills. The curricula or lessons that have been previously learned should be reviewed from a concrete point of view. Teaching sequences should begin with familiar concrete ideas that can be explained through demonstrations, hands-on activities, manipulative objects, and so on. Introducing something abstract to early adolescent students without a concrete base rarely works in getting the concept across. Students who are good at memorizing information may memorize a concept and how it works and might appear to understand it but will not necessarily internalize it.

In introducing a new principle, rule, or definition, give concrete examples and show application before stating the rule or principle. For example, do a science experiment (or have students do it) so that they can see what happens during the course of the experiment. Then discuss the principles or theory behind it. In this way, the students can relate the theory or principle (abstract) to the experiment they just observed and experienced (concrete). Then questions of interpretation and analysis can be asked to determine what the experiment means and how it applies to another situation. Questions that can be posed might begin, "What if . . . ," "How do you know . . . ," or "Are you sure . . ." Students must follow a line of logic or reasoning to explain the answers. In this way, they are guided through the thinking process from concrete to abstract in a step-by-step fashion. Examples of resources that can be used to illustrate the concrete include charts, pictures, photos, manipulative objects, films, and demonstrations.

The teacher also needs to verbalize the thinking process to early adolescent students. When discussing a new principle or concept, talk through the sequence of ideas or steps aloud or make a chart of the sequence. This will enable students to follow your logic and line of thinking as well as see the progression of your thinking so that they can understand the process and model it themselves. Also, when they are answering questions or giving explanations about abstract types of things, ask students to verbalize their thinking, to justify and explain their reasoning to you and the class. Others in the class will then be given an opportunity to follow the student's thought patterns. When students appear to be going off track, redirect them so that they can try again.

# MIDDLE SCHOOL CURRICULUM

The middle school curriculum should not be treated as a mini high school curriculum but rather as an entity of its own. Too often in the past, the middle school (or junior high school) curriculum was just that: a mini high school curriculum where abstract concepts in physics, chemistry, and math, for example, were studied and where the use of logic and abstract reasoning was often required in many subject areas. As we have seen, most early adolescents are not able to think formally. When students are introduced to thinking skills beyond their realm of comprehension, understanding, and capability, they become frustrated and do not do well, often developing a dislike for a subject that stays with them for many years. Once again, students with good memories might do well by memorizing but may not internalize the concepts or reasoning presented.

During the past decade, many strides have been made in developing and revising the curriculum to make it more appropriate to the characteristics and needs of the early adolescent intellect. Middle school curricula should serve as a transition between elementary and high school curricula, combining characteristics from both. The content and subject matter of the middle-level curriculum should serve as a vehicle for the development of the many processes and skills appropriate to the changing nature of the early adolescent intellect. Examples of these skills include the teaching and development of study skills, note-taking skills, research skills, and information-processing skills. These require the use of both knowledge and process, and each has a tangible (or concrete) aspect as well as some intangible (abstract) aspect. The development of these skills provides a solid foundation of skills for secondary-level studies.

Developing a strong base of information-processing skills is an important part of the middle-level curriculum and a necessary part of preparation for future learning. If students learn only to memorize information and subject matter (concrete), they may forget it by the time they reach high school. However, if students develop a sound base of information-processing skills, they will be able to work with any subject matter and content in future learning situations more effectively and with greater ease. Therefore, in addition to studying facts and information, students need to develop or solidify skills of using information. An important goal of education today is to develop self-directed learners who can be responsible for their own learning in our fast-paced society and ever-changing world.

Research skills such as locating, accessing, organizing, and classifying information can be developed through increased emphasis on project-type work or activities in almost any subject area. Note-taking and study skills can be developed by practicing skills such as looking for the main idea, sequencing, and summarizing. Many of these skills involve working with information but using it in a semiabstract way.

The period of academic slowdown that occurs during the middle school years (during ages 12 to 14) must also be considered in the development of learning materials. This, coupled with many other changes students experience, means that they should not be pushed beyond their academic capabilities during these years. For the majority of students, early adolescence is not a time for great academic strides. One of the most important goals of middle-level education is to have early adolescents make significant strides in personal and social development as they become young adults. Thus, during the middle grades, academics must be balanced with affective educational concerns.

## PLANNING LESSONS AND ACTIVITIES

Because of the restless nature of early adolescents and the well-known problems of classroom management and discipline, the preplanning of lessons and activities for early adolescents is very important. Good planning and good classroom management are inevitably tied together. Good planning leads to meaningful, logical, and interesting lessons. Students need to be informed of the goal of the lesson, how it relates to previous lessons (when applicable), and how it will relate to future lessons. Unplanned or poorly planned lessons in an early adolescent classroom can be disastrous. Students with no sense of direction or those who finish activities before the class is over are candidates for getting into trouble. This can easily lead to multiple discipline problems.

Because of student restlessness and shortened attention spans (15 minutes) and concentration levels (8 to 10 minutes), a variety of instructional methods should be used with early adolescents throughout the day as well as within specific lessons. Pupil achievement is positively related to situations where a variety of instructional methods, technologies, activities, resources, and materials are used. This factor needs to be considered when designing lessons. Examples are lectures, demonstrations, hands-on activities, individual work, group work, audiovisual presentations, cooperative learning, pupil–teacher planned activities, and field trips. Strategies can be used from the expository mode, such as explanations, lecture, discussions of printed materials, and use of a textbook, as well as from the inquiry mode, including questioning, investigations, experimentation, field trips, and group problem solving.

Peer tutoring can work effectively at the middle level. Peer tutoring involves pupils teaching or assisting other pupils in an area of the curriculum where they need help. Through peer tutoring, the pupils who need help can get it, while those who teach their peers benefit from the leadership role it provides. In these situations, many academic skills as well as social dynamics and other skills in the affective domain are learned.

A variety of resources can be used in planned lessons. Examples are audiovisual materials (videos, tape recordings, slides, filmstrips), computers, manipulative objects (for example, science equipment), charts, and posters. A variety of evaluation methods such as written tests, oral tests, observation of students, interviewing of students, student work, student journals, student self-evaluation, anecdotal reports, behavior logs, and checklists can also be used with students.

Providing structured opportunities for group work and peer interaction on a regular basis can be used both as an instructional strategy and for social skill development. Lessons involving group work must be guided and directed activities, otherwise they can easily degenerate into nonproductive socializing.

## MOTIVATING EARLY ADOLESCENTS

Motivating early adolescents is not always easy. They are easily bored and distracted, and academic subjects are not always high on their list of priorities at this time in their lives. In addition to these factors, teachers cannot compete with the drama and flair of the media for entertaining children and holding their attention. While each student differs in his or her level of motivation, there are several techniques that classroom teachers can use to assist with the motivational process.

First, a sense of humor can be used as a motivational strategy. A bit of humor injected into dry subject matter can make it more interesting and can move things along. In addition to humor, a sense of showmanship and drama can add interest to a lesson from time to time. For example, a teacher can get dressed up in the costume of an era that relates to a history lesson (such as a war soldier or a town crier). Props related to the topic under study can be brought in to add interest to a lesson. For example, when studying the lives of pioneer people, bake or bring to class some cornbread to illustrate a staple in their diet. Bring your slides from Australia to class when teaching a unit on Australia. Tell interesting stories about your travels as they relate to relevant subject matter. A little imagination now and then can go a long way.

Allow students some freedom of choice in selecting the topics for their activities and work when possible and appropriate. If students choose a topic of interest to them, they are more likely to do well and to stick with it. Varying lesson formats and instructional strategies as discussed previously can also help to make motivation less of a problem.

Relevance is another important motivational factor. Early adolescents have difficulty identifying with situations that cannot be shown to have some relevance in the here and now. As a result, the more personal a lesson is made and the more relevant it can be shown to be to contemporary situations, the more interest and participation will be generated among students. For example, when studying the government's introduction of taxes to the colonies in a social studies lesson, discuss why taxation is necessary, the kinds of taxes we pay today, and what they are used for. Look for opportunities to bring relevance to a lesson whenever one presents itself. Use examples, problems, and points of illustration that relate to student concerns and interests at this level. Relevance makes lessons more interesting and meaningful to students.

At times, motivation may be a problem because a child is troubled or lacking in the basics of life. For example, the child may be hungry, or he may be exhausted from lack of sleep or from working too many hours at a part-time job. The child may be abused or preoccupied with difficult family situations. Do not overlook these factors as a reason for the lack of motivation in individual students.

## IDEALISM AND FANTASY

As they begin to view the world from a more adult-like perspective, early adolescents tend to be idealistic. As a result, they are very vulnerable to fantasy and often have difficulty distinguishing between reality and fantasy. The middle school level is an appropriate time to have students begin to think critically about what they see, hear, and read about in the world around them.

Changes in technology over the last few decades have brought about many new forms of mass media and communication technologies. Because of the pervasive nature of the media in society, it affects our culture and shapes our values and norms. The images and information presented in the media can also affect our beliefs and attitudes and can ultimately change our behaviors. While this is the case for adults, it is even more so for children and young adults. Most television programming and movies are created for adults and not for children. While there are programs developed specifically for children, as they get older, children usually watch more adult programs, videos, and commercials. Advertisements and programs geared to adults often distort reality or idealize certain aspects of adult lives. Examples are idealizing sex, drugs, and prostitution as well as glorifying violence. Programs and movies also frequently deal with the theme of romantic love.

During early adolescence, children are particularly vulnerable to fantasy and idealism as they explore the adult world for the first time. Adults view things in the media as fantasy, but this is not always the case with early adolescents. Lacking experience with adult life, their perceptions of adult life are often formed and influenced by what they see in the media. As a result, many early adolescents develop unrealistic expectations of life and then become disappointed, depressed, and prone to poor self-esteem when their lives don't measure up to their expectations, as portrayed in the media. Not realizing that the images in the media are highly idealized and unrealistic, many students attribute the disappointment about their expectations to the fact that something is "wrong" with them, their lives, or their circumstances.

Early adolescents need guidance in the use of the media. While the value and benefits of the media can be taught (for example, the media is a tool for mass communication and a source of entertainment), early adolescents need to be made aware of the fantasy in the way messages are often presented. Early adolescents need to realize that although the settings, images, and people in commercials, movies, videos, and magazine advertisements appear real, they often do not represent real-life situations. Rather, they are distorted images of reality designed to entertain people and influence consumers. Early adolescents need to realize that things are not perfect in the real world and life is not *always* wonderful, fun, and exciting as the media might have people believe. In reality, people don't change their looks overnight because they use a new shampoo, nor do they run across open meadows to embrace the boyfriend of their dreams. Early adolescents need to see and understand the symbolic messages behind the media settings and messages.

Teachers and educators can help early adolescents learn to deal with the media by helping them learn to recognize it for what it is. This can be done by providing opportunities for critical studies of the media in terms of its purpose, value, effects, and influence on our lives. Critical-thinking and analytical skills, which early adolescents are beginning to use, can be used to explore and explain the themes and fantasies portrayed in the media. Of course, it should be noted that the media is not "bad" but that it's nature should be understood realistically.

An effective way for teachers to approach media study and analysis in the absence of preexisting programs is to make use of television programs, commercials, videos, and magazine advertisements that students are accustomed to seeing. Students can be asked to review a media piece and do things such as look for the meaning or message that advertisers are trying to get across (for example, if you use this face cream, you will be beautiful; if you drink this kind of beer, you will have fun), decide whether the messages are realistic, and determine why advertisers use the format they do to get the intended message across.

## OTHER CHARACTERISTICS OF THE EARLY ADOLESCENT INTELLECT

Early adolescents are curious individuals, and they love to experiment and explore. They prefer to be actively involved in learning situations rather than participate as passive observers. This needs to be considered when designing lessons and learning activities. The hands-on approach, where students can work with materials on their own in structured situations, is an effective teaching strategy provided it is guided and directed by the teacher. For example, instead of talking about what happens to magnets when their poles are brought together, design lessons that allow students to experiment and discover it for themselves. To promote active learning, early adolescents can also be engaged in lessons in which they are urged to build, design, and illustrate.

Early adolescents have vivid imaginations. Through experimentation and exploration, they can be very creative and generate innovative projects and approaches. They do need encouragement and support, however, because of their self-consciousness as well as a general lack of confidence. Opportunities to express their creativity can be provided in classes in creative writing, art, music, computer use, and many others.

## EXPLORATORY EDUCATION

Exploratory education is another feature of middle-level education that helps early adolescent students discover and identify individual interests, abilities, talents, and potential. This is done by providing students with opportunities to "explore" a wide variety of activities and learning experiences outside of traditional subject areas such as math and science. While the structure and content vary from school to school and district to district, exploratory programs support the early adolescent need for exploration and experimentation and take advantage of their frequently changing interests.

Exploratory curricula traditionally included subjects known as "unified arts" (that is, art, music, industrial arts, and home economics). While many of these subjects are still part of exploratory education programs at present, programs today can also include high-interest minicourses, electives, and activities (such as craft design, drama, first aid, career planning, wood carving, and block printing), as well as independent study and enrichment activities based on areas of individual student interest. Students typically take courses or electives for one period a day for 6, 9, or 12 weeks at one grade level. Courses and activities can be required, elective, or a combination of both depending on the school district's program requirements.

# 13

# Teaching and Physical Development

Early adolescent bodies are rapidly changing ones. This rapid growth and development, which results from sexual development and the pubertal growth spurt, has implications for the development of curricula, lesson plans, and teaching strategies in the middle-level classroom.

As a result of variations in physical weight and height among early adolescent students, a variety of desk sizes (and other equipment) should be available in each class to physically accommodate every student. Two students who are the exact same chronological age can have vast differences in height, weight, and stature. Some students may need to change desk sizes several times over the course of the year. Other students experiencing temporary myopia (short-sightedness) may need to move closer to the front of the class in order to see more clearly until the problem corrects itself.

Middle-level teachers must be careful to ensure that early adolescent bodies are not physically overstressed. While at times students have abundant energy, they can also tire easily during growth spurts. Problems such as exhaustion can occur as a result of periods of disproportionate growth of muscles, arteries, heart, and lungs. Intense physical activity should be avoided during these times.

Because of rapid bone and muscle growth, restlessness is a common problem for early adolescents. Uneven growth and development makes sitting for long periods of time difficult. Lengthening bones and changes in muscle cells result in a need for movement. Organize schedules and lessons so that students have opportunities to move periodically, to relieve some of the restlessness.

Awkwardness and clumsiness is another outward sign of a rapidly changing body structure. Be prepared for the consequences of this development in the classroom. Because of student awkwardness, things will accidentally get pushed and moved around or broken from time to time. Plan to have extra items on hand to replace any vital equipment that may get broken (for example, have extra beakers on hand in science class). Students are very self-conscious about their awkwardness and clumsiness, and teachers should not single them out or embarrass them about it.

## SEX EDUCATION AND
## SUBSTANCE ABUSE PROGRAMS

During the middle school years, children experience the process of puberty, which ultimately results in sexual maturation. Most students who come to the middle school are aware of the basic concepts involved in sexual development and reproduction. In spite of this, however, they do not have a firm base of knowledge or a realistic picture of all that sexual maturity entails, particularly because of the sexual behavior they observe frequently in the media. Studies indicate that the peak time for the implementation of sexuality education is during the middle school years. Because early adolescents are experiencing sexual development, they are very curious about the process.

Most states now require that classes on human growth and sexuality be implemented in middle schools. While the approach to sex education varies from state to state and district to district, today it is much more broad based in scope than it was in the past. No longer consisting of a study of animal reproduction or the biological facts involved in the physical act of human reproduction, programs on human sexuality today are comprehensive. They include a wide range of topics related to sexual development such as child birth, contraception, sexually transmitted diseases (such as AIDS or venereal disease), teen pregnancy and its consequences, peer pressure regarding sexual activity, responsible decision making, responsible sexual behavior, and sexual assault. In a society continually bombarded with numerous kinds of sexual stimuli and innuendo, early adolescents need to have accurate information about sexuality and to learn about responsible sexual behaviors. The purpose of a comprehensive sexuality curriculum is to provide middle-level students with accurate information concerning sexuality, which will, in turn, enable them to make healthy and responsible sexual and relationship decisions.

Early adolescent students need to understand the process of sexual development as it relates to their own bodies during this time in their lives. They also need to understand that the sexual feelings they have are normal. The psychological dimension of sexual development is important. Young adolescents need to develop a healthy acceptance toward the developmental changes they are experiencing, and they need to know that the process of sexual maturation is a perfectly normal one. Middle-level students are often anxious about their development, particularly when it is out of step with their peers or is different from others in any way. They need to be reassured that all children go through puberty but that each does so at his or her own time and pace. They need to know that just because they are ahead or behind their peers in development does not mean that something is "wrong" with them.

Teachers must be aware of the impact and anxiety that the process of physical growth and sexual development generates in early adolescents. A classroom teacher can play an important role in this regard by recognizing this type of anxious behavior in students and providing reassurance about their fears and insecurities, particularly when opportunities to do so arise within the context of the normal teaching day. For example, a physical education teacher who observes that Jeffrey is getting very frustrated with himself because he can't seem to kick a soccer ball as accurately as he did earlier in the year can take the boy aside and say something like, "Jeffrey, I can see that you are frustrated with your skill in kicking the soccer ball lately, but this is a normal and only temporary change. Your body is growing and changing very quickly right now, and that is why you don't seem to be doing as well as you once were. Don't be too hard on yourself in the meantime. Keep playing and trying. The skill will eventually come back once your growth slows down."

Repetition of information about physical growth and sexual development is needed during the middle years. This is because when the material is initially presented, students who have not yet begun development are not usually as receptive to, and retentive of, the information as those who are experiencing rapid growth when the material is being presented.

A substance abuse curriculum is also mandatory in most schools today. Experimentation with drugs, smoking, and alcohol often begins during the middle-level years. During early adolescence, students are vulnerable to experimentation as a result of their curiosity, the urge to explore, the desire to imitate adult behavior, feelings of invincibility, and peer pressure. Current substance abuse programs focus not only on identifying potentially harmful substances and explaining the biological effects of foreign chemicals in the body and on the brian, but also on related topics. These can include why people use drugs, how drugs and alcohol affect people's behavior, social problems related to substance abuse (such as violence in the home, crime, and poverty), and how to deal with peer pressure and substance abuse.

While the classroom teacher may or may not be responsible for the implementation of sex education and substance abuse programs, teachers need to be aware of the content of the programs and how they are implemented. Questions from students who seek answers or informal counseling on these matters can then be dealt with in an appropriate manner.

Students are extremely self-conscious about their growth and development. If there is a need to speak to them about it, it should be done discreetly so that the student is not embarrassed. Students are also very sensitive about any physical markings that are unique to them such as moles and birthmarks. Any focus on, or discussion of, these should be avoided.

## MENSTRUAL PROBLEMS

Middle-level teachers need to be aware of common menstrual problems girls experience during early adolescence. Teachers, both male and female, must recognize that many girls will experience their first menstrual period during school hours. This can be an upsetting time for these girls, especially for those with a limited understanding about what is happening to them. Reassurance and understanding from the classroom teacher can be extremely helpful. A male teacher who is made aware of the situation can discreetly involve the school nurse or another female teacher who knows the student. Students who experience the unexpected arrival of their menstrual period will need to be excused from class. It is common for the first few menstrual periods to be irregular until the menstrual cycle becomes established.

Teachers should also be aware that the most common cause of absenteeism among early adolescent girls is menstrual pain (dysmenorrhea). Studies suggest that two-thirds of early adolescent girls experience dysmenorrhea at some time, usually soon after the onset of first menstruation. Pain and cramping during menstruation were originally thought to have psychosomatic origins. This myth and others about menstrual cramping, such as the assertion that menstrual pain occurs as a result of a lack of exercise, too much stress, or having a low self-concept, have been proved untrue by research. Menstrual cramping is a problem of biological origin and must be taken seriously. Teachers need to be aware of it and must be prepared to deal with students experiencing menstrual-related problems in the classroom.

## PHYSICAL DEVELOPMENT AND SUBJECT AREA CONCERNS

The physical and biological development of early adolescents warrants special attention in several subject or curricular areas. These are to be considered in addition to the implications of intellectual characteristics and development discussed earlier.

### Physical Education

The implications of physical development on curriculum and lesson planning are perhaps greatest in the area of physical education. While early adolescents at a particular grade level can be the same age, there are usually great differences in the level of physical development attained by individual students within a class. Some students may not have begun the growth spurt and sexual maturation process, whereas others can be nearing the end of the process. This variation, as well as the rapid rate at which growth and development occurs during puberty, must be considered in the development of curricula, lesson plans, and activities for middle-level students.

In all types of athletics, variability in the rate of growth and sexual maturation of students dramatically affects their abilities. Developmentally advanced students have the advantage over those who are just beginning their growth spurt. As a result, competitive sports and activities among early adolescents can be unfair and frustrating to late maturers. These students feel inadequate when they are not chosen to be on sports teams or are always chosen last. Early adolescents become extremely frustrated when they cannot compete or excel in sports because of limited physical size and growth over which they have no control. Thus, physical activity involving competition with others should be downplayed and self-competition encouraged. This can be done by focusing on skill development in sports and activities that involve individual skill development and self-competition. Some examples include bowling, skiing, skating, archery, golf, swimming, orienteering, and dance.

During early adolescence, health-related problems in physical education can arise if physical activity during rapid growth spurts is not moderated. With the heart and arteries developing behind the rate of growth of other body parts, blood cannot always be pumped fast enough throughout the body to accommodate the needs of an energetic early adolescent. With the heart, muscles, and lungs growing at disproportionate rates, students should be closely monitored for any sign of physical stress and exhaustion. Overtaxing the system with excessive and intense physical exercise during this growth stage can be dangerous.

Another problem caused by differences in the rate of development of various body parts is clumsiness and a lack of physical coordination. The acceptance of a lower level of skill ability and proficiency is often necessary during times of rapid physical growth for this reason. Students just begin to adjust to a specific movement with some precision when growth and change elsewhere in the body causes them to have to readjust. Teachers can provide understanding and encouragement to these students during these times of frustration or as the need arises.

It is important to recognize that in addition to all of the usual health-related reasons, physical education is necessary during early adolescence to provide an outlet for the excessive restlessness that characterizes students of this age group. Differences in the rate of physical development between the sexes (girls develop faster than boys) must also be recognized and accommodated.

Teachers must also be aware of the self-consciousness and embarrassment students feel in the shower and locker rooms because of advancement or lag in physical or sexual development.

Students are particularly aware of their changing bodies during this period, and those who develop earlier or later than others or are different from the norm in any way are often teased or harassed. Teachers need to be aware of this in order to help to prevent it from becoming a problem for the students who are vulnerable.

## Music

In the subject area of music, the physical and biological aspects of early adolescent development that must be recognized and accommodated when planning lessons and activities are changing voices and rapidly changing physical coordination. Early adolescents, especially boys, often hesitate to sing because they are embarrassed about the sound of their changing voices and are afraid others will laugh at or make fun of them as a result. While early adolescents prefer to listen to music (music appreciation) rather than sing, singing activities involving groups of students (including school choirs) are preferable to individual activities such as solo performances. Students will feel more secure and will not feel as embarrassed or afraid to sing if they are part of a group singing effort. In this context, they feel they won't be noticed or singled out. As a result of changing voices, students may also have difficulty with certain voice exercises (singing scales) during early adolescence. Musical activities requiring the use of fine-motor skills (playing instruments) may be difficult or not suitable for early adolescent students during periods of rapid growth.

## Home Economics, Shop, and Technology Education

While home economics and shop as subjects are now recognized by different names (family studies, industrial arts) or are integrated into broader curricular programs (technology education), they include many activities that involve physical dexterity and the use of machines and other electrical equipment and appliances. Because early adolescents can experience difficulty with coordination, accidents can occur at any time with the use of this equipment. Safety must be of utmost consideration in the development of programs for these subject areas. Safety rules must be clearly explained to students and strictly enforced. Students may also have trouble from time to time working on skills that require good coordination and dexterity as a result of their rapid and uneven growth.

## Art

Poor physical coordination can be problematic in middle-level art classes, particularly with work that requires the use of fine-motor skills. The early adolescent view of art tends to be one of "realism"; therefore, students try hard to imitate or reproduce things in art exactly as they see them or exactly as they are in reality. When their efforts result in immature artistic impressions or work that does not measure up to their idealistic or perfectionistic expectations, they become critical of their work and discouraged. As a result, middle-level art students need plenty of encouragement, recognition, and approval. Clumsiness and awkwardness are often responsible for breakage (pottery), spillage (paint), and other similar "accidents" that can occur in the classroom when using raw materials and equipment. Because of early adolescent restlessness (as well as rapidly changing interests), art projects that can be completed within a relatively short period of time are more suitable than those requiring long stretches of time.

## Computer Education

Once again, early adolescent awkwardness and clumsiness means that computer equipment needs to be located away from high-traffic areas, cords should be carefully secured to the floor or wall, and so on. Equipment such as keyboards and monitors also need to be secured in place to avoid "accidents" while students are using computers. Computer skills requiring fine-motor skills (typing) can be difficult for students experiencing rapid physical growth.

# 14

# Social and Emotional Development and Teaching

Teachers and educators have an important role to play in shaping a child's social and emotional development during early adolescence. It is a role that requires as much attention as academics and one to which teachers must devote a great deal of care, concern, and understanding. In middle-level education, the social and emotional (affective domain) development of early adolescents is considered as important as academic (cognitive) development.

Early adolescents are in the process of becoming young adults. During childhood, they developed social and emotional skills that served them well and that were appropriate to their needs at that time. Children are keenly aware of adult roles and abilities, and they can make a clear distinction between themselves and adults. Recognizing themselves as children, they act like children and rely on adults for emotional security and well-being as well as for guidance and direction.

As children become physically mature young adults, they eventually realize that they are no longer children and that acting like children is no longer appropriate. They recognize that they need to act more like adults in areas of social and emotional development. However, with a child-like perception of adult lives and no experience in being adults, they don't know how to go about doing it. For the early adolescent, there are no books or people or any other source that tells them exactly how to act like an adult in the many circumstances in which they find themselves. While books and resources can help, early adolescents generally learn to act like adults on their own with the guidance of significant adults in their lives. During the process, they often feel uncomfortable and they make many mistakes. Making the transition from childhood to adulthood in the area of social and emotional development is therefore difficult.

Through their observations of the behavior of adults around them and through imitating adult behavior, early adolescents eventually begin to develop the skills they need to become young adults. Often the behavior they model is that of adults in the media, whose lives appear glamorous and filled with fun and adventure.

As early adolescents experiment with adult behaviors and try out adult roles, they are very insecure and unsure of themselves. They constantly question themselves as to whether they are doing the "right" thing or acting the way they are "supposed to" act. They also worry about what others think about their new behaviors. Consequently, early adolescents are plagued by self-doubt and self-consciousness. In attempting to cope with new feelings and behaviors, they experience many emotional ups and downs. This being the case, the role of significant adults who can provide them with positive feedback, guidance, direction, and reassurance throughout the process is very important.

## AREAS OF SOCIAL AND EMOTIONAL DEVELOPMENTAL NEED

Early adolescent social and emotional development includes many areas of growth. Early adolescents have to develop an identity of their own and discover how they fit into society. They have to learn self-acceptance and need to develop a positive self-concept and positive self-esteem. Their concepts of themselves, their families, and their peer relationships undergo great changes, and they need to make the adjustment to these changes emotionally and socially. Students need to grow morally and develop a sense of ethics; to become more self-sufficient in order to become independent persons and independent thinkers; and to learn to accept responsibility. They need to learn how to get along with others, how to act with members of the opposite sex, and how to act in various social situations. They need to learn courtesy and proper etiquette to direct their behavior in social situations, and they must become self-sufficient in the area of proper grooming. The development of sportsmanship, skills of cooperation in working and dealing with others, and leadership skills (academic, social, or athletic) is important, as is the development of interpersonal communication and conflict resolution. They need to recognize their own creative abilities, to express themselves as unique individuals, and to develop an aesthetic appreciation of art, music, and drama.

This list is by no means complete. Early adolescent needs in the area of social and emotional development are numerous—too numerous to discuss adequately in the limited space provided here. Indeed, entire books have been written on many of the individual aspects previously mentioned (for example, self-esteem). Our discussion of early adolescent social and emotional needs will be basic and general as a result. Teachers can expand and build on concepts presented and can explore these areas in much more depth by using available resources.

## FOSTERING SOCIAL AND EMOTIONAL GROWTH

An important part of the middle-level teacher's role is facilitating the social and emotional development of early adolescents by guiding and directing them through the process of becoming young adults. In a true middle school, the social and emotional needs of early adolescents are considered in the development of all aspects of student life: in the development of the overall curriculum, in the physical organization of the school and individual classrooms, in the development of student schedules and classes, and in the development of extracurricular programs and social activities.

Social and emotional development can be addressed both formally and informally at the middle level. It can be formally addressed through the implementation of programs or curricula designed specifically for the purpose of developing social skills and enhancing emotional development. Examples are a guidance unit on the topic of peer pressure or a unit on developing a conscience. Through these programs, various social and emotional needs of early adolescents are directly addressed.

Skills can also be developed indirectly through a traditional curriculum in which opportunities for group work, social skill development, and student interaction are integrated. For example, after a science lesson on the environment, students work in small groups to plan ways to improve the environment around the school grounds.

The third method of formally addressing the social and emotional needs through the curriculum is also an indirect method. Students are provided with opportunities to discuss issues related to affective development through existing or traditional curricula or programs. An example is having students discuss how a character feels about being a social outcast in a novel under study in reading.

Social and emotional skill development can also be achieved informally in the school setting. Teachers can assist in this process by modeling adult behavior in the classroom and by guiding, directing, and helping individual students with many of their social and emotional problems and concerns that are not serious. A more complete discussion of the role of the teacher as a counselor and adviser to students is found in Chapter 15.

# WAYS TO FORMALLY ADDRESS SOCIAL AND EMOTIONAL DEVELOPMENT

Aside from formal programs and curricula that teachers may be expected to implement, there are other things that can be done within the context of the existing curriculum to foster social and emotional growth among early adolescents.

First, in planning lessons or academic units for use in the classroom, include some learning objectives from the affective domain. For example, when studying a war in a social studies class, have students imagine and discuss what the feelings of the soldiers might have been or how war affects people's personal lives and the lives of their families. In a novel under study, have students analyze a social or emotional situation involving a particular character. For example, ask questions such as, "Do you think Joe's behavior was appropriate? What would you have done if you were faced with his dilemma?" In a unit on substance abuse, discuss not only the facts and information as they relate to the substance but also how substance abuse affects peoples lives, their relationships, their work, and so on.

In physical education classes, discuss the concepts of sportsmanship, teamwork, winning, and losing. Students need to develop an understanding of these concepts from a more adult perspective.

In music and art classes, introduce students to the concept of aesthetic appreciation. Discuss the purpose of music and art, the role of music and art in society, and what a piece of music or artwork conveys to those for whom it was created.

Develop activities that provide opportunities for student self-discovery, self-analysis, and self-understanding. For example, in a creative writing class, have students write about what they want to be when they become adults, focusing on why they made their choice as well as the reason they think they would be good at it. Have them write about some aspect of their hobbies or talents and why they like them.

To foster independence and to have students develop a sense

of responsibility, allow them opportunities to make their own choices and decisions. Teach students that in making their own choices and decisions, they must accept the consequences of their actions and choices.

One of the more common ways to foster social growth in the classroom is to create opportunities for peer interaction through group work. This can be done within the context of the existing curriculum. One of the goals of affective development at the middle level is to have students learn skills that will enable them to work successfully with others in a group situation. These skills can be developed through providing opportunities for structured and directed group activities as part of everyday learning. For example, instead of providing pencil-and-paper or textbook-generated activities for students to work on individually after a lesson or series or lessons, make a point of developing some group activities to reinforce what has been taught.

Group activities should be directed and structured. As we previously discussed, early adolescents are preoccupied more with social needs and activities than with academics. Both excessive talking and socializing are among the most common discipline and classroom management problems in the middle-level classroom. Early adolescents naturally seek out this type of behavior whether opportunities are present or not. It is important, therefore, that group-oriented activities be well planned and thought out in advance by the teacher. Clear directions and expectations need to be given to students so that they are aware of exactly what is to be done during the activity. A timeline should be provided so that students know what is expected within the allotted period of time. Task organizers outlining what is to be done in a step-by-step fashion can also be used. Activities can involve small groups, larger groups, or students working in pairs. It is important to provide training and instruction in group participation skills. For example, discuss the need to take turns talking and the need to respect others' opinions. Discuss the role of various individuals working in the group setting. Outline the responsibilities of the group leader, the group recorder (note taker), and the other members. Do not assume that students can do these things on their own until they have had considerable practice.

Participation in after-school activities or extracurricular groups where students can socialize and take part in nonacademic activities in a positive setting is to be encouraged among students. These settings provide further opportunities for students to develop social skills. The ability to select their own leaders and to participate in organizing their own activities in this setting is important. Teachers can encourage participation by praising and supporting groups of students involved in positive after-school activities. After-school activities provide teachers with opportunities to observe and compliment students on skills and activities that are not necessarily academic in orientation.

There are many well-written novels specifically for and about early adolescent lives and problems. Teachers can use these as resources to indirectly help students deal with the many adjustments they are required to make during early adolescence. The use of these books can be integrated into existing curricula, programs, or specific lessons, when appropriate. They can also be recommended to students for recreational reading, or teachers can read aloud to the class during time set aside for this purpose. By reading these books, students often gain insights into their own lives and characters. The books usually revolve around conflicts typical of early adolescent children such as peer problems, the need for acceptance, early adolescent frustrations, awkwardness, and growing pains. Most early adolescent students can relate to the characters of the books and how they feel because they have similar feelings themselves. They can also read about how many problems of early adolescent characters are solved. A list of some of the more popular of these books is provided at the back of this book. It may also be useful for teachers to read some of these books themselves from time to time to become familiar with the early adolescent psyche and with the kinds of problems and feelings they experience. It should be noted that the availability of these books for use within the classroom is dependent on school or district policy. In some districts or schools, all books used in the classroom must be approved (usually by a committee) before they are used. The teacher needs to be aware of the school policy, as it may not be possible to use the books listed in all schools.

## WAYS TO INFORMALLY FOSTER SOCIAL AND EMOTIONAL GROWTH

There are numerous ways that a teacher can foster social and emotional growth and development in the classroom on an informal basis. Many of them have already been discussed in other contexts in previous chapters.

First, teachers need to be aware that they serve as role models for the students they teach. While this is the case for students of all ages, it is particularly important at the middle level when students are making the transition from childhood to adulthood and looking to adults as models for appropriate behavior. Teachers need to be aware that their behaviors and attitudes, both conscious and unconscious, can effect the students they teach.

Teachers of early adolescents can foster social and emotional growth by modeling, discussing, and explaining the adult way of doing things to their students. Acting like adults is a new experience for early adolescents. We often assume that students will learn to act like adults on their own. While this is true to some degree, early adolescents need to be taught about proper adult behavior. Many early adolescents today do not have good adult role models in their personal lives and home environment. Many are misled about the nature of adult life by what they see in the media. And most of them still have somewhat immature perceptions of adulthood they have carried over from childhood. Teachers can help students sort through these misperceptions through modeling, discussion, and explanation. For example, if students are to act responsibly, we have to talk to them about responsibility—what it means to be responsible and how to act responsibly in various situations. If students are to be good sports in playing with others on various teams, we must tell them how.

Students cannot know how to act by imitating adult behavior alone because much of the adult behavior early adolescents try to model is portrayed unrealistically in the media. When early adolescents do try to model appropriate adult behavior, they are unsure of themselves. Students need guidance and direction in addition to appropriate models to follow. They need to hear about adult behavior from a reliable source. They need a foundation to work from—something to fall back on when they don't know how to act and they find themselves in circumstances where they have to act like an adult. While many students already demonstrate a good understanding of adult behavior as a result of having a good example set in the home or elsewhere, many other students have no such understanding. Guidance and discussion will benefit these students most and can serve as reinforcement to those who appear to be doing well in this area.

An important note needs to be made about how to go about explaining adult behavior to early adolescent students. Because early adolescents tend to have a "know-it-all" attitude, it is advisable to use a low-key approach. Although early adolescents think they know it all, they obviously don't. Therefore, the messages and information we want to pass along to them about adult behavior need to be conveyed in a subtle way. If the information is given in a condescending manner, students are more likely to reject what is said or develop a rebellious attitude toward it (for example, "That teacher thinks we are babies and that we don't know anything"). The "I'm the adult and I'm going to tell you how to act" authoritarian approach should be avoided.

A low-key approach in which the discussion of adult behaviors is integrated or infused into the curriculum or classroom discussions works best. Using characters in stories and novels under study provides an excellent forum, as do news items, a film, or a television program. Using suitable personal examples and anecdotes as a springboard for this discussion from time to time can also be a good way to get the message across.

Of course, students will not always appear to appreciate any information provided for their benefit, but it is mainly because they want to appear as if they already know what you are telling them. This suggests another way to approach a conversation about adult behavior; that is, begin the discussion with a sentence like, "I know many of you already know this, but we're going to review it anyway. . . ."

While guiding and advising them, teachers must recognize that most often, early adolescents learn by trial and error. Early adolescents need to discover and experience things for themselves. No amount of information or experience we can provide for them as adults will entirely eliminate that need. What we can do to help is guide them through the process by sharing our ideas and knowledge with them in a nonthreatening, collegial way. Then we need to allow students to make their own decisions and mistakes, providing that the student's safety is not involved. Early adolescents will then learn to accept the consequences of their decisions and actions as well as learn to accept responsibility.

Once again, contrary to the appearance that early adolescents no longer need or want adults as they increasingly assert their independence, they have a very strong need for security. The entire world of the early adolescent is based on change. For this reason, they have a strong need for a secure environment. Although they seldom express it, having a stable and secure classroom environment with a teacher who is caring, understanding, and responsive to them is important and brings them a great deal of security and satisfaction.

## BUILDING SELF-ESTEEM

One of the most important things a teacher can do during the middle-level years is to help students build a good self-concept and positive self-esteem. Students with positive self-esteem have a strong sense of belonging within their families, their peer group, and society. These students acquire positive self-esteem when they are successful; when they feel competent; when they accomplish, achieve, or earn a goal; and when they feel accepted and valued.

Because early adolescents experience so much change in so many areas of their lives over a short period of time, and because they are constantly experimenting and trying out new roles to establish an identity of their own, they don't really know who they are. Because the early adolescent perception of himself is always changing, early adolescents are insecure and vulnerable. Self-esteem during early adolescence is also tied in part to factors outside of the child's control (for example, physical attractiveness, intelligence, money, and possessions). For these reasons, it is difficult for an early adolescent to develop a good self-concept and positive self-esteem. In the human life cycle, self-concept and self-esteem are at their worst during early adolescence, particularly between ages 12 and 15.

Parents and teachers increasingly recognize the importance of a good self-concept and positive self-esteem in children. However, many teachers and parents are unclear or misguided in their understanding of how self-esteem is acquired. A popular misconception is that self-esteem is built by frequently praising a child or by telling a child that he is good and therefore he should not feel bad about himself. For children who have nothing to feel good about, this kind of talk can appear insincere or patronizing. On hearing such comments, some students think to themselves, "You don't know me very well, or you wouldn't think that I'm good." Sincere praise is no doubt important, but it is only part of the overall process of building self-esteem. It can rarely work on its own without the other essential components. Another popular misconception about self-esteem is that it is acquired when children receive lots of attention or when the child is made happy.

Self-esteem is something a child has to feel. It is a feeling that comes from within and grows within a child. It has to be built and fostered over time. Self-esteem is not something that can be given or told to a child. It is not external, but internal. While external factors can support or contribute to its growth, self-esteem originates from within an individual. A child has to believe that he is competent and valued, that he can achieve and accomplish, that he is loved and worthy. Only he can feel these qualities. There are many ways that an adult can help a child to develop these feelings, but ultimately it is the child who must internalize them.

Building self-esteem is multifaceted task. It requires providing the tools a child needs to feel competent and to become successful. It involves identifying a child's strengths and helping her build on them. It requires providing recognition, encouragement, and praise for a child in her endeavors, and it includes making a child feel valuable by showing a genuine interest in her and in demonstrating care, compassion, and understanding.

Self-esteem is also something that takes time and consistent effort to build. It cannot be done overnight, in a week, or in a month. It cannot be done with a single program or a single statement. It is an ongoing process that takes place over an extended period of time.

Early adolescents who have the best chance of developing positive self-esteem are those who have the love and support of their parents and the support of their peers, their teachers, and other significant people in their lives. A child who lacks support in one of these areas is at some risk. Those with no support from any of these areas are at the greatest risk.

It is in the best interests of educators and teachers to help build self-esteem in early adolescents because research demonstrates a positive relationship between positive self-esteem and school success. Students with positive self-concepts are more likely to finish high school, to get better grades, to participate in extracurricular and social activities, and to be less influenced by their peers. Students with negative self-concepts tend to do poorly in school, are more subject to peer pressure, and have difficulty with friends and school work.

Having said that, it must be noted that while students with good grades and other positive skills usually have positive self-esteem, it does not mean that this is always the case. For example, students who tend to be perfectionists may get good grades and exhibit model behavior but still have low self-esteem because they aren't "perfect." For example, Jackie got her social studies test back and burst into tears because she got a grade of 88 percent. Another student might be thrilled to get this grade, but Jackie usually gets grades between 96 and 100 percent, so she interprets this lower mark as a failure. Thus, while the low self-concept and poor grade correlation is common, it is not limited to students with low grades.

## WAYS TO BUILD SELF-ESTEEM

There are many ways that teachers can help to build self-esteem in middle-level students. Some of these have already been discussed previously in other contexts but bear repeating here.

1. Identify areas of student strength. Help and encourage students to develop the skills they have in these areas so that they can experience success with them. Developing competence and experiencing success builds self-esteem. Each student has different strengths. For some, it is academics, while for others it can be in athletics, art, music, community service, or other areas. Students do not always recognize their strengths and talents. During the middle school years, teachers can help to put students in touch with their strengths and can provide encouragement to develop areas where they demonstrate talent.

2. Get to know students by name. Get to know their interests. Ask them about their hobbies, interests in sports, and so on. Welcome them back after a period of absence. This makes students feel that you have a genuine interest in them, and they feel valued as a result.

3. Recognize and praise positive behaviors. Look for opportunities to praise students whenever you can, and always do it in a sincere manner. There is something about each student that warrants a compliment from time to time. Make it a point to look for these things to help boost self-esteem.

4. Provide a positive classroom atmosphere. A classroom that is stable and secure will help a child feel physically and psychologically safe. A child also needs to feel a sense of belonging in the classroom, and he needs to feel that everyone is treated fairly.

5. Treat all students with dignity and respect, and never use putdowns, sarcasm, and other messages that say, "You're no good." That does not mean that a teacher should never reprimand, scold, or criticize the behavior of students when it is warranted. It means it should be done in a manner that is not humiliating or belittling to them. For example, Daniel is found cheating on a math test. To deal with the matter in an appropriate manner, the teacher might approach the situation as follows:

TEACHER: I'm very disappointed to see that you cheated on your math test, Daniel. I know very well that with effort you could have easily passed the test without cheating. You have passed all of your other tests in the past, and you certainly have the ability to pass this one, too. By cheating, you are defeating the purpose of testing in education. I can't tolerate this behavior. It is not good for you and not good for others. I'm going to assign you a grade of zero for this test, and I am going to call your mother and tell her about it as well.

An inappropriate approach and one to be avoided in this situation is as follows:

TEACHER: So . . . You cheated on your math test. Well, frankly that doesn't surprise me, Daniel. You've been in so much trouble around here lately, and you just don't seem to ever do anything right. You know, if you keep going at this rate, you're never going to amount to anything.

6. Be understanding of the changes that each student is experiencing, and be sensitive to student self-consciousness in all areas of development.

7. Recognize and reward successes in social development. If rewards or awards are given for academic achievement, have them for social skill development and improvement as well (for example, perfect attendance, good manners).

8. In writing reports or giving any other formal feedback to students, point out the good with the bad. Do not overwhelm the student with negatives only. It is a good idea to start and finish with a positive comment.

9. If possible, get students involved in community service projects. Positive feedback from the community or positive press coverage can contribute to increased self-esteem for each student involved. For example, take the school choir to perform an informal concert at a home for the aged, or take the drama club to a nursery school to put on a play for the children. Have students plant trees for an Arbor Day project. Students will get positive feedback from the audiences involved and will feel a sense of accomplishment for what they've done for others. There is a positive relationship between participating in community service projects and positive self-esteem.

10. Structure learning experiences and the classroom environment in a way that will generate as much success as possible for students.

11. Encourage students who do not do well academically to become involved in extracurricular activities, sports, and after-school clubs where they will have opportunities to experience success in other socially approved settings. This can reduce the possibility that they will seek success by turning to negative behaviors and/or to peer groups where negative behavior may be condoned and applauded.

12. For students who do not excel, reward their efforts. If they are trying hard and appear to be doing their best, compliment them for their efforts and encourage them to keep trying to do their best. If they are not capable of doing any better, it is futile to pressure them further. Unnecessary pressure will only cause stress, frustration, and lower self-esteem.

13. Help students set and assess their goals realistically. For example, when a large number of students want to be on the school basketball team, tell them that only a limited number of students can make the team and that just because a student doesn't make the team doesn't make him a failure or any less of a person.

14. Help students sort through faulty thinking that reflects a misinterpretation of events. The way in which a student interprets situations, as well as his accompanying thought patterns, can have a significant effect on student self-concept and self-esteem. For example, Louis and Bob are "average" students. Their marks are very similar, as is their good behavior in class. Louis has low self-esteem, and Bob has positive self-esteem. We can examine their thought patterns to see why this is the case.

BOB: I study and work hard. I'm not doing as well as Sam and Steve, but when I try hard, I seem to do OK. My parents are happy with my performance and so is the teacher, so I'm happy with myself, too. I'll just keep trying to do the best I can.

LOUIS: No matter how hard I try, I can't seem to do as well as Sam or Steve. It's no use. I don't know what to do. I guess I'm just no good.

Louis's thoughts are unrealistic because he assumes that he can somehow do better than anyone else all of the time without taking into account ability or various other factors. He also assumes that because he cannot do better than Sam and Steve, it means he is no good or a failure. He feels that if he can't do as well as Sam or Steve that there is no use in trying. He is using Sam's and Steve's standards to measure his own. On the other hand, Bob is more realistic in his thoughts in that he recognizes that not everyone can be at the top of the class. He knows that he is doing as best he can in relation to his efforts and ability, and he can feel good about himself as a result. Students need to be aware that their thought patterns can affect the way they feel about themselves. Irrational thought patterns need to be recognized and changed.

## PEER PRESSURE

Peer pressure affects people all through life, but it is strongest during early adolescence. During early adolescence, a child's acceptance by peers is important for psychological well-being. Most early adolescents belong to a peer group, and many belong to more than one peer group at a time. These peer groups vary in size, interests, social background, and structure.

One of the main reasons early adolescents want to belong to a peer group is for security. Because they are so unsure of themselves, early adolescents find security in numbers. In conforming to and following the standards of those in a peer group, early adolescents feel safe. The group provides a place for early adolescents to try out new roles, behaviors, and ideas. It also serves as a source of feedback on their beliefs, values, attitudes, and behaviors from people other than authority figures or adults. In belonging to a group and being accepted and recognized by its members, early adolescents gain a sense of self-esteem.

Being part of the peer group, however, means conforming to its standards. Students conform to the standards and pressures of their peers in order to be liked, to feel accepted, and to fit in with others. When group standards or pressures concern things that are harmless (such as dress, musical tastes, hairstyles, or speech), there is no danger in belonging to the group or conforming to its standards. Peer groups can be a positive force on children by pressuring them to do well academically and keeping them away from misbehavior. However, when peer pressure is applied to get students involved in negative behaviors (such as drugs, alcohol, sex, cheating, stealing, and behavioral misconduct), it becomes a negative influence in the student's life and then becomes a problem.

Peer pressure during early adolescence is clearly linked to student self-concept and self-esteem. Children who feel good about themselves and their accomplishments are more confident, have a sense of self-respect and integrity, and feel worthwhile. Children with positive self-esteem are less afraid to stand up to others and are better equipped to resist going along with others.

Children with poor self-concepts and poor self-esteem often don't like themselves and feel worthless. They are more likely to be influenced by peers and to conform to peer pressure because they fear ridicule and rejection. They lack the confidence to be different and to walk away from a situation that makes them uncomfortable.

## HELPING STUDENTS OVERCOME PEER PRESSURE

What can teachers do to help students overcome peer pressure?

1. Build self-confidence and self-esteem in students as previously discussed. It is clear that students with positive self-esteem are less prone to pressure from their peers than those with poor self-esteem.

2. Discuss the concept of peer pressure with students. They need to know what it is, how and why it exists, and how it affects their lives so that they can recognize it. Tell students that peer pressure is strongest at their age and explain why. Many students do not recognize that the pressures they feel to follow the crowd are those of peer pressure. Many also do not realize that most of their peers are experiencing the same feelings that they are. With an understanding of peer pressure, students can assess its impact on their lives and learn strategies to cope with it. While programs and curricula that deal with peer pressure are available in some schools and districts, in the absence of formal programs, teachers can do much on their own to educate students about the topic.

3. Develop or implement problem-solving and decision-making activities based on various scenarios related to peer pressure. The long-term consequences of peer pressure can then be studied objectively when the student is not "on the spot" or not in a situation where she is being directly confronted with peer pressure with no time to think about consequences. Students can discuss and share their ideas on managing peer pressure. In this way, they can also see that there are many ways that problems can be approached and dealt with. Early adolescents also need to

know that it is all right to say "no" when they are uncomfortable with a situation. The information discussed by students in these sessions will provide material or information they can fall back on if they do find themselves in a situation where they are being pressured to do something against their will or judgment and have no time to think about it. The development of general problem-solving and decision-making skills also helps early adolescents manage peer pressure more effectively.

4. Encourage students to get involved in extracurricular activities and after-school groups where they can meet their need to socialize and where they can experience a sense of belonging in a positive group setting.

5. Recognize and compliment students in peer groups for their good or prosocial behavior from time to time so that others will be encouraged to do the same.

6. Do not allow any negative aspect of peer pressure to exist in the classroom. For example, don't allow students to put each other down in front of peers. Emphasize that each student in the class is to be treated with respect and that behavior such as ridiculing and name calling will not be tolerated.

## STRESS

Stress is something that everyone experiences to varying degrees throughout life. In recent years, much has been written about the ill effects of stress and its relationship to disease. In our fast-paced and rapidly changing society, stress and stress-related disorders are on the rise.

Stress is also on the rise among early adolescents. Early adolescence has always been a stressful period for children, but with many of the added pressures and stresses of today's society (such as drugs, violence, and family instability) and less support from traditional support systems (such as church, family, and a stable community), stress among early adolescents is greater than ever. One of the major causes of stress is a lack of control over one's life and environment. During early adolescence, children have no control over their growth and development. In addition, many are unprepared for the changes they experience or do not understand it. Puberty then becomes a very stressful period for them to endure.

Stress also results from anxiety. Early adolescents have many anxieties as they try to cope with continuous change and with many new and unfamiliar experiences. There are four or five general areas in which early adolescents experience stress and anxiety. School is one area. Students feel they are under pressure to get good grades and to do well in school. They find taking tests and getting projects and assignments done on time stressful. Getting along with teachers and administrators and staying out of trouble are also concerns for some.

A second source of stress and anxiety is friends and peer relationships. This includes making friends, belonging to a peer group, being liked and accepted by peers, and experiencing peer pressure.

A third area of stress is family life. Getting along with brothers, sisters, and parents is a source of stress. Family instability, parental divorce, moving, and family crises can also be concerns.

The fourth source of stress is developmental change: adjusting to the physical, emotional, social, and intellectual changes involved in the process of puberty. Examples of concerns in this area are being a late or early developer; worrying about appearance (that is, hairstyle and clothes); worrying about how to act and behave in various social situations and with members of the opposite sex; and dealing with sexual awakening and new emotions.

A fifth category of early adolescent stress can include a variety of other concerns such as fear of nuclear war, fear of crime and violence, environmental concerns, and so on. Early adolescents having to cope with stresses from all of these areas can easily be overwhelmed by the changes and anxieties they face. While many students are able to manage their way through this difficult period, some are overwhelmed by it and feel a sense of helplessness, powerlessness, and a loss of control.

A good self-concept and positive self-esteem are key factors in determining a student's ability to cope with the many stresses he or she faces every day. Students with positive self-esteem have the confidence to withstand and overcome many situations they are faced with and are better able to keep their spirits up and solve problems in spite of difficulties. These students feel that they have some control over situations in their lives. Students with negative self-concepts and negative self-esteem do poorly at handling stress and anxiety. They often feel that situations are totally out of their control and that they can do nothing about them. As a result, when these students are overwhelmed, some turn to alcohol and drugs as an escape or as a means of coping with their lives and its stresses. They do not have the foresight to see that these are not solutions and will only prolong the need to deal with stresses and problems over the long run. Some students can also become seriously depressed.

When students perceive that they are totally powerless and that there is no hope left, some turn to suicide as a solution. These students perceive everything in their lives negatively and see no hope of ever getting out of their anxious, stressful, or depressed state. Suicide is currently the second largest cause of death among adolescents in America. The largest cause is accidents, which unfortunately includes fatalities that often result from substance abuse. Students usually talk about suicide and think out how they will attempt it before they do. It is absolutely crucial that any student who speaks of suicide in any way be immediately referred to a professional (such as a school psychologist or social worker) for help.

Early adolescents need to understand what stress is and how it affects them in order to learn how to cope with it. They need to understand that stress can be controlled, reduced, and in some cases eliminated when certain measures are taken. Through the implementation of guidance programs or curricula that deal with the topic of stress, students can learn to recognize the symptoms of stress and learn coping strategies and skills. Through these programs, which are often implemented by classroom teachers, students learn to minimize the negative effects of stress, learn how to use moderate stress to their benefit, and learn coping strategies such as relaxation techniques and problem-solving skills to help them cope more effectively with stress in their lives.

It is important for middle school teachers to monitor students, identify those that appear to be under too much stress, and intervene and provide assistance or referrals to professionals when necessary. While it is not always easy to tell if a student is just experiencing the normal ups and downs of puberty or if he is experiencing too much stress, a teacher can watch for patterns in the intensity and frequency of certain behaviors exhibited by students. Some of the most common behaviors or signs include explosive episodes of crying, irritability, aggressive or self-destructive behaviors, and frequent self-deprecating statements. Teachers should also monitor students who show signs of substance abuse or a decline in achievement, students who withdraw socially, and students who are unable to concentrate. Students may engage in these behaviors as a way of either coping or not coping with too much stress. The problems that early adolescent children experience usually manifest themselves behaviorally before they are discussed or expressed verbally. The teacher must use her knowledge and experience with individual students to determine whether the behavior is the result of too much stress or just typical early adolescent behavior. Conferring with colleagues as to their observations of the child can often help in these situations.

## HELPING STUDENTS COPE WITH STRESS

Aside from the implementation of guidance programs on stress and stress management, there are other ways that teachers can help students deal with stress on a day-to-day basis in the classroom:

1. Build self-confidence and self-esteem. Students with a sense of worth and self-confidence are much better at coping successfully with anxiety and stressful situations.

2. Provide support when students appear to be overstressed. For example, let a student vent his frustrations or let out emotions by asking him what is troubling him.

3. While acknowledging student disappointment, tell students that disappointment doesn't feel good, but it is a normal feeling for people to experience. Tell them that everyone is not always happy with the way things work out and that it is unrealistic to expect that things will work out all the time. One disappointment does not mean that things won't be better another time or that everything is bad because of one disappointment. Encourage students to look for alternatives on the issue on which the disappointment is based, and encourage them to move on to other things, if or when appropriate.

4. Help channel defeatist and distorted self-talk and thinking. For example:

STUDENT: Because I got an F on my math test, I'm no good.

TEACHER: Just because you failed a math test, Isabel, doesn't mean that you're no good. It means you failed a math test. You did pass all your other tests, and you have been doing well on the volleyball team. You also have many friends, so how can you be no good? You shouldn't tell yourself that you're no good. Tell yourself that next time you'll try harder or that you're bound to do better if you show more effort.

Show the student that she has control over her feelings by how she interprets things and by what she thinks and says to herself. Students need to know that feelings don't come out of nowhere. Although they can't control events, people can choose how they feel about them. By helping students make more appropriate interpretations of things, behavior should become more adaptive and less self-defeating.

5. Help students deal with unrealistic expectations. This can

be done with individual students or with the class as a whole. For example, study advertisements and their messages in class to identify how they promote perfection and ideal lives that are unrealistic.

6. Provide quiet time in the classroom during stressful times (or on a regular basis). During quiet time, students can relax by reading a book, putting their heads on their desks for a few minutes, or engaging in other relaxing strategies to break the pace.

7. Help students better manage their time so that the causes of stress related to poor time management (that is, not getting projects done on time) can be reduced or eliminated.

8. Help students learn to accept themselves for what they are (self-acceptance). Tell them that we all are unique—we each have our own qualities, strengths, and weaknesses. Some of us are not good at school work but are good artists. Others may play sports well but cannot sing. We need to accept what we are and work with our strengths. It is because each of us is unique that we can work successfully in society. Society needs a diverse population in order to exist and function. People with a variety of strengths are needed to fill all of the necessary roles in society (such as teachers, mechanics, and musicians).

9. Tell students not to worry about things too much. This is especially important as it relates to their self-consciousness. Tell them that other students their age are worried about the same things as they are. For example, ask students to think about whether their fellow classmates are worrying about what to wear, how they look, and whether they said the right things.

10. Teach problem-solving skills in the classroom, and use them to help students help themselves with their problems. Explain that everyone has problems and that they are a normal part of life. For this reason, students need to learn to solve problems. Explain that sometimes we think our problems are so great that no solution can be found, but almost every problem can be handled if broken down into manageable pieces. The best way to deal with problems is to face them head on. Tell students that running away from problems is no solution because the problem

will usually follow and will not go away. Students who don't face problems or who try to solve them by turning to drugs and alcohol as an escape are not solving anything. They are just creating another problem in the long run. Tell students that they can learn to solve problems, and if they are having trouble with a problem, they should ask for help from a reliable adult source.

11. For individual students experiencing temporary stress, engage them in an activity that diverts their attention away from stress for temporary relief.

12. Be alert to symptoms of stress in students, and invite communication in a private and dignified way. Refer students whose stress is causing serious problems to a professional for help. Refer anyone talking of suicide immediately.

13. Have students acknowledge that no one is perfect, that we all make mistakes, and that making mistakes is all right if not done intentionally and if we learn from them.

14. Help students with perfectionistic tendencies to be more realistic in their expectations of themselves and in their interpretations of things. They need to accept the fact that no one is perfect and that making perfectionistic demands of themselves subjects them to unnecessary stress. They need to realize that they don't need to be perfect to be a good person or to be accepted by others.

# 15

# The Teacher as Counselor

An important goal of middle-level education is to foster healthy emotional and social growth and development. Because early adolescents experience so much change in the area of emotional and social development during the middle years, there is an increased emphasis on the role of guidance to meet the increased demand. In the middle school, both teachers and specialized staff share the responsibility for providing guidance services for students. Therefore, teachers who work at the middle level must be prepared not only to teach academics, but also to act in an advisory or counseling role to students. This does not mean that the middle-level teacher assumes the role of a "professional" guidance counselor or any other professional whose specific role it is to perform counseling services (for example, a social worker or a school psychologist). In no way does the use of teacher advisers reduce the need for trained professionals in this area. Rather, teachers and professional counselors work together. Early adolescents seem to have many problems coping with the daily stresses and strains that result from some aspect of developmental change. Problems that are not of a serious nature can be dealt with by middle-level teachers and do not require "professional" help. To adults, many of the problems and concerns of early adolescents seem trivial, but to early adolescents, they are very real and need to be addressed. The early adolescent need for help and guidance is often immediate. Teachers are in a good position to respond to these needs as a helping adult friend.

## THE HOMEROOM PERIOD

At the middle level, most schools have an established homeroom or homebase period or an adviser–advisee program. Through these programs, each student spends part of every day with the same homeroom teacher or teacher adviser. During these homebased periods, time is provided for nonacademic interaction between the homeroom teacher and the students. Formal lessons or traditional subject matter (such as math and science) are not taught during these periods. However, the time can be used to implement an affective domain curriculum such as a guidance program. The time can also be used informally so that students are free to approach a teacher with questions or concerns they may have while other students in the class work on an informal task (for example, doing homework, planning a field trip). Because students spend time with the same teacher every day in this setting, both teacher and student have an opportunity to get to know each other fairly well, and a relationship builds between them as a result. Under these circumstances, students are more likely to feel comfortable approaching a teacher for advice. The purpose of the homebased period (adviser–advisee program) therefore is to provide early adolescents with a support base to help them with the transition from the secure, self-contained one-teacher classroom of the elementary school to the multisubject, multiteacher structure encountered at the high school. It also provides an opportunity for teachers to get to know a number of individual students well. It then becomes easier for a teacher to recognize changes in a student's behavior that may signal the need for help or professional counseling. The teacher can also use her knowledge of the individual students in her class to help other teachers and professionals in the building understand and deal with a particular child more effectively.

## COUNSELING ROLES OF THE TEACHER

The middle-level teacher has three general roles as a counselor. One of them is recognizing serious problems with individual early adolescent students and making referrals to appropriate professionals when necessary (such as a school nurse, social worker, guidance counselor, or school psychologist). The next role is that of counselor or adviser to parents, that is, educating parents interested in knowing about early adolescent development and behavior. The last role involves acting as an adviser or counselor to students on a day-to-day basis on matters of a less serious nature.

### The Teacher as Referral Agent

Middle school teachers must be alert to serious problems plaguing individual early adolescent students so that they can be referred to appropriate professional personnel for help. Sometimes a student's problem is obvious, but other times she may be troubled with problems that are not obvious. There are many signs that can indicate a student may be having problems and may be in need of assistance. Teachers need to be aware of them and need to watch for them as they work with students every day. Examples of behavior that can signal underlying problems include the following:

1. There are significant changes in a student's behavior. For example, a student is normally outgoing but has become very withdrawn over a period of time, or a normally well-behaved student begins to act out frequently.
2. There is a significant drop or change in a student's grades or academic performance. For example, a student who is

normally a "B" student suddenly begins failing tests or getting "D" grades.

3. A student frequently appears nervous. For example, she is fidgety, loses her temper easily, bites her nails continuously, or engages in sudden emotional outbursts for no apparent reason.

4. A student appears to be experiencing psychosomatic problems. For example, he has frequent stomachaches.

5. The student appears distant, inattentive, and lethargic, and she spends much time looking out the window or with her head on the desk.

6. The student makes many negative statements about himself. For example, "I hate myself" or "I'm no good."

7. The student appears to have no friends his age or begins to have significant peer problems (for example, he is constantly threatened by a bully).

8. The student has trouble concentrating or doesn't complete work.

9. The student appears to be constantly frustrated.

10. The student looks sad and depressed most of the time.

11. There are signs that a student is engaging in some form of substance abuse (for example, he has alcohol on his breath).

12. The student talks about suicide or dying. In this case, it is necessary to refer her immediately.

There are other circumstances when referring a student may be appropriate:

13. The teacher is aware that a student is having significant family problems. For example, the child's parents are divorcing, and she does not appear to be coping with it well.

14. The student's parent has requested she be referred for a particular reason (learning or behavior problems).

15. The student asks a question or asks for advice on a topic with which you do not feel comfortable. In this case, ask

the student if she would like you to refer her to someone more appropriate.

Because many of the above-mentioned behaviors can be considered normal or typical early adolescent behavior, it is not always easy to detect behavior that is indicative of underlying problems. However, important indicators to look for are a distinct or sudden change in behavior and behavior that becomes constant or very intense. When teachers know their students well and monitor student behaviors over time, it is easier to recognize when student behavior is attributable to normal early adolescent behavior or when it might be a reflection of a more serious problem.

If a teacher suspects that a student's behavior is indicative of an underlying problem, he needs to initiate contact with the student and then must refer the student to the most appropriate professional available. To do this, the teacher needs to be familiar with the professionals available in the school and community and their respective duties and responsibilities regarding student counseling.

### The Teacher as Counselor to Parents

The middle-level teacher also serves as a counselor and resource person to parents seeking advice about a child. Many parents are unaware that a child's behavior can be related to the physical and biological changes they experience during early adolescence. For those who express a concern or those who are interested, teachers can review the developmental changes with parents and explain how development affects a child's behavior. They can also recommend books or articles for parents to read that can provide further information on the topic.

Parents can also seek a teacher's advice on managing a child's behavior. When requested to do so, the teacher can share information on behavior management with parents. At times, parents having trouble managing a child might ask the teacher to recommend a professional who can help, or they might ask the teacher to make a referral to a professional.

## *The Teacher as Student Adviser*

The guidance role of a middle-level teacher is to serve as a counselor or adviser to early adolescent students with minor problems that can occur on a day-to-day basis. In this role, the teacher can meet the needs of students in two different ways: through group counseling and through individual counseling.

Group counseling is often done in conjunction with the implementation of guidance and other affective domain-based programs. While guidance personnel implement some of the programs related to social and emotional development, often they are too busy looking after their formal individual student counseling duties as well as other administrative tasks. Thus, in many schools some of the responsibility for implementing the guidance curriculum falls on the classroom teacher. These guidance programs are usually focused on issues concerning the social and emotional development of early adolescents and include things such as adjusting to changing bodies, developing a conscience (values education), developing communication skills, making responsible decisions, learning conflict resolution tactics, and so on. These programs are developed largely to help students better understand themselves. In some schools, they may also include programs that focus on health education issues, substance abuse, and mental health and well-being. The teacher implementing these programs in the classroom does so during the homeroom period or during the adviser–advisee program with the same group of students on an ongoing basis, over the course of the year. The teacher serves as a leader and counselor to students on issues addressed in the programs and can advise students individually or in small group settings.

An important part of the implementation of these programs is getting students involved in discussions on the topics presented so that students have an opportunity to reflect on the material and think about how it affects their lives. In this setting, increased opportunities are provided for peer interaction and cooperation, the development of decision-making and problem-solving skills, and the development of leadership skills. Group discussions also provide opportunities for student self-analysis, critical-thinking skill development, and the development of debating skills, among others.

The teacher's role as day-to-day adviser and counselor to individual students consists largely of giving students time and attention with everyday problems and expressing care and concern for student welfare and well-being. The teacher need not wait until the student expresses an obvious problem. The teacher will observe many problem situations in the classroom over the course of the day or week in which students simply need encouragement, reassurance, or a kind word. An important part of the teacher-as-counselor role includes identifying these situations and making appropriate comments to students in need of support, particularly as the matter relates to the building of self-confidence and self-esteem. It is just as important for a teacher to offer support to insecure early adolescent students as it is to deal with student counseling.

The most common situations that teachers deal with in their adviser–advisee programs are questions and concerns from students regarding personal, social, and educational problems. Personal problems can concern difficulty in coping with changing bodies and individual student concerns about normalcy. Early and late developers in particular often express a great deal of anxiety concerning their development or lack of it. Students may also become frustrated during the growth spurts when skills they used successfully in the past no longer produce the desired results. In these cases, students need a great deal of reassurance about their situations.

A student's home life must also be taken into consideration if he is having problems at school. Because of the strong need for security in their lives, parental divorce or family instability can be more devastating and detrimental during early adolescence than at any other time in their childhood lives. This can lead to increased emotional and behavioral problems in the classroom. Teachers need to be aware of the impact these conditions can have on a particular child, and they need to be sensitive to the child's needs as a result. Showing interest and concern to children experiencing difficult situations at home by being compassionate and making supportive statements can be very helpful. In some instances, because of ongoing problems at home, coming to school and talking with someone who cares can be the highlight of the day for some children.

Examples of social problems include various aspects of learning to get along with others. For example, "Kenny always thinks he's the boss. He takes over the game and tells everybody what to do and I'm getting tired of it." Other examples include being teased by others, being unpopular, coping with various social situations, and having arguments with friends that end in tearful displays of emotion. In this case a teacher might say something like, "I can see that you're very upset, Leanna. Is there something I can do to help?" or, "Having an argument with a friend doesn't mean the friendship will end or that the person doesn't like you. All of us have disagreements with others from time to time, but we still remain friends." Remember that active listening is important during these times.

Academic concerns can be expressed by students having difficulty adjusting to the middle school environment. This includes the inability to cope with different subject areas taught by different teachers during the course of the day and questions about which course electives to choose and which extracurricular clubs or sports teams to join. Students often need help in identifying and clarifying their strengths, special interests, and aptitudes. Students may also need help with homework or independent study projects.

Sometimes unusual or unexpected situations arise in the classroom and need to be addressed. When this happens, subject matter needs to be put aside in order to deal with the concerns at hand. For example, if a student in the class has just experienced the death of a parent or sibling, the student's friends as well as others in the class will feel very uncomfortable on hearing about it. They will not know what to say to the student or how to act with the student when she comes back to school. They may feel a sense of grief themselves. In this case, the teacher needs to take time away from the lessons of the day and discuss the matter with the class. If the teacher is uncomfortable about the situation or unsure of how to proceed in dealing with it, she can consult a professional in the building (such as the school psychologist) about ways to approach the situation or what to say to students about it. When students are very upset by an incident of this nature, it is unlikely that they will be able to pay attention to formal lessons.

One other important note about student counseling: Many schools have policies that dictate the type of counseling concerns that should and should not be dealt with by classroom teachers. Each teacher should be familiar with this policy where one exists or should seek advice from administrators when in doubt.

## COUNSELING TIPS

In working with students on a daily basis and counseling and advising them on problems and concerns, the following are some tips that teachers can use:

1. Never dismiss or trivialize a problem that a student brings to your attention. For example, a student tells you, "Everybody laughs at me because they say my nose looks like a beak." Treat all problems as important. Any question or problem considered important enough to be brought to the attention of a teacher by a student needs to be addressed. Never make fun of a question or put down a student who asks it.

2. In dealing with early adolescent problems and concerns, it is sometimes helpful to put yourself in the shoes of the child in a given situation in order to see things from his perspective and to have a better understanding of his problem.

3. Some students will want to ask a question but may be too shy or embarrassed to ask it in an outright manner. Very often, these students will "beat around the bush" or talk around it. This

is common among students of this age. When this happens, try to facilitate the situation insofar as it is possible. Help the student get the question out without embarrassing her. Some teachers keep a question box at the back of the classroom in which students can deposit their questions anonymously. Questions are then answered by the teacher at a specified time (for example, at the end of the day, on Fridays).

4. Recognize that talking things out with students is usually very helpful even though it may not appear that any good has been done.

5. Active listening is important. Many times, a student does not want advice but just needs to vent his frustration about a situation. Allowing students to release their emotions and get whatever is bothering them out of their system is often therapeutic. In these cases, being an attentive listener and lending a shoulder to cry on may be all that is necessary. Even if advice is sought, when a teacher listens rather than talks much of the time, the student gets the impression that the teacher really understands his concerns or situation. Being an attentive listener is one of the most important things a middle-level teacher can do in a counseling role.

6. When a student asks for advice or suggestions, try not to solve the problem for her. Rather, help the student solve the problem, or direct her in a manner needed to solve her own problem. This can be done, for example, by asking a series of questions. It is also important to emphasize to these students that problems can be worked out with some thought and time.

7. Be alert to symptoms of stress in students, and motivate them to talk about it if possible. While early adolescent students are often reluctant to share and discuss feelings, the student is more likely to feel comfortable enough to discuss a problem with a teacher when a trusting relationship has been established. Underneath student reluctance often comes a sense of appreciation of the fact that someone cares about them. If a student refuses to discuss a problem, do not force the situation.

8. Provide encouragement and support to students who

need it without necessarily getting involved in individual counseling. Some students simply will not ask questions or ask for advice, but it is obvious that they need support and reassurance. Early adolescents are very insecure and need continual support from adult sources in the face of constant change. As you recognize a need, give your support. Build confidence and self-esteem whenever an opportunity presents itself, and do it in a sincere manner.

9. As a homeroom teacher, get to know your students and take an interest in them on an individual basis early in the year. Study their habits and personalities. Ask them questions about their favorite hobbies or sports teams. Not only does this build a good rapport with the student, but with a better understanding of each student, it becomes easier to recognize when his behavior is out of character or when he is having difficulty later on. Knowing a student's personality also provides a base for making decisions on how to handle his behavior. It also provides direction as to the approach to take when counseling him.

## PARENT CONFERENCES

Teacher–parent conferences at the middle level are held for many of the same reasons that they are held at other educational levels: to report on a child's academic progress, to inform the teacher of a change in family or health status, and to resolve behavior and other related problems. Because of the many changes experienced by early adolescents during the middle years, teacher–parent conferences and discussions often take on a slightly different orientation. While parents are usually more concerned about their children during the middle school years, at the same time, they are generally less informed about early adolescent development and behavior. Many parents know that their children will eventually become rebellious and moody and will display many of the behaviors typically associated with early adolescence. However, they expect the behavior to begin at a later age, typically when children are teenagers. Thus they are sur-

prised and sometimes shocked when the behavior begins to surface in their children as early as 10 years of age.

Parental reaction to the process of puberty and the changes in
a child's behavior during early adolescence varies from parent to
parent. Some parents take it in stride, while others become frustrated with their child and his behaviors. Some of these parents
may turn to the school and teacher for help and suggestions to
better understand and cope with the early adolescent child.
Comments from these parents typically include, "I can't seem to
handle him at home anymore. He won't listen to a thing I say. I
don't know what's wrong with him, and I don't know what to do
about it."

Other parents are caught off guard when they receive a phone
call or letter from the school about a child's dropping grades or
negative behaviors. In many of these cases, it is happening for the
first time since the child began attending school. Parents generally
appreciate being informed of a negative or deteriorating situation
with their child, and they will usually intervene. Some parents
notice changes in their child's behavior at home and are not
surprised that it has surfaced at school as well. However, a few
parents will react with disbelief on such notification, perhaps
because the child's negative behavior has not yet surfaced at home
or the child acts differently at home (the two-personality syndrome discussed earlier). As a result, these parents may believe
that changes in the child's behavior are not attributable to anything the child has done, but rather insist that it is due to a "bad"
teacher, an inappropriate curriculum, a new administrator, and
the like. Typical comments from these parents include, "Derrick
never got into any trouble at school before. Someone must have
pushed him into it" or "Janet never failed a math test before.
Maybe the teacher is no good." These parents reason that since the
child has not been "bad" or done poorly academically in the past,
she will not do so in the future. Thus, they reason that an
explanation for the child's behavior must lie somewhere outside of
the child and not within the child's own actions or control. While
these and other factors for a child's poor performance must be
considered by teachers in assessing the reason for the child's

problem, most often the behaviors occur as a result of developmental change. Many parents do not make the connection between developmental change and differences in their child's behavior. It is understandable, then, that if a child has been well behaved at home, a parent will find it difficult to comprehend why the child is different at school. With these parents, it is important not only to make them aware of the child's problem but to educate them about early adolescent development and the possible impact it may have on the child's behavior.

This leads to the main difference between teacher–parent conferences at other levels of education and those at the middle level. At the middle level, a good deal of the teacher's time at parent conferences is spent educating parents about early adolescent development and behavior. Most parents appreciate the time a teacher takes to explain developmental changes, and they appreciate the recommendation of any articles or books they can read on the topic. However, there will always be a few parents who will refuse to accept explanations and will continue to insist that something is wrong with the teacher, the curriculum, the teaching methods, the new principal, and so on. Do not take the insinuations or negative remarks personally in these few cases, and work with the child as best you can for the rest of the academic term. If it is appropriate, you might ask the parent if she would like to speak to the curriculum coordinator or the principal about her concerns.

When a lack of parental cooperation occurs, it is unfortunate because one fact about teacher–parent conferences remains clear: When a teacher and parent work together to help a child, their efforts are far more likely to succeed than when one or the other is trying to work on it alone. Good relations with parents is therefore very beneficial to both teacher and child.

## PLANNING A TEACHER–PARENT CONFERENCE

When a teacher–parent conference is successful, it is because the teacher plans for it and has the skills to conduct a successful conference. When a conference is unsuccessful, it is usually because it has not been well planned or the teacher lacks the necessary skills to conduct a good conference.

The purpose of having a teacher–parent conference is to share information and to discuss concerns that are for the benefit of the student. A conference can be called by either the teacher or the parent. During a conference, the concerns of the participants are discussed and plans are made to improve a problem or area of concern, when necessary. Many districts require that a specific number of teacher–parent conferences be held during the year (most often one or two). These are usually held to discuss student report cards and general progress. Other conferences can be called spontaneously to deal with any problems or concerns that arise.

There are basically three types of conferences. The first is to deal with a specific problem a child is experiencing. The second is to get acquainted with a child's parents, family background, and health or to allow parents to become acquainted with their child's teacher. The third is to share information on academic and behavioral progress.

In some circumstances, conferences can also include the presence of the school principal, vice principal, school psychologist, social worker, and student. When planning or setting up a conference, there are several things that need to be considered:

1. The conference should be scheduled in advance so that those parties involved have sufficient time to prepare and plan for the conference. In the case of the teacher, allow enough time to prepare what is needed for the conference (for example, student records).

2. The conference should have a definite purpose. Develop an agenda based on that purpose. Use it during the conference to ensure that each point you intend to make is covered in a logical and orderly fashion. The agenda need not be anything elaborate. An outline written in point form on a scratch pad should suffice if you will be the only one using it.

3. Plan what needs to be done or said at the conference ahead of time, and prepare the necessary documents accordingly. In

addition to an agenda, have available student files, workbooks, report cards, anecdotal records on behavior, test results, and anything else you may need.

4. Choose a quiet location with a pleasant atmosphere that is free from disruptions and disturbances for the conference.

5. Assist parents in finding solutions to mutual problems by asking questions such as "Can you think of any way we might work together to resolve the situation?" If the parent does not have any suggestions, or if you are asked for your suggestions, propose your alternatives and solutions. Possible solutions should be thought out ahead of time, whenever feasible. Emphasize the importance of working together.

6. Make a few notes about the conference for your records *after* the parent has left. For example, make notes on the agreed-on course of action, write a reminder that a referral needs to be made for the child, or make notes for a follow-up meeting or letter.

7. Plan the course of action, if one was agreed on during the conference, and then act on it. Keep records on the progress made so that those involved can be informed of the progress (or lack of it) at any future meetings and inquiries.

Other useful tips for conducting teacher–parent conferences include the following:

1. Greet the parent in a friendly manner.
2. Be tactful and diplomatic but truthful when discussing problems with the parent. Back up what you say by using facts and data (such as test results, behavioral diaries). Try to keep opinions to a minimum, or wait until an opinion is asked for before expressing one.
3. Discuss and exchange information during the conference. Refrain from lecturing.
4. Use a positive approach. Don't bombard the parent with a lot of negatives all at once. Make a point of beginning and ending on a positive note.
5. Be a good listener. Allow the parent to state her case, and allow her to vent frustration when necessary.

6. Be clear in your speech. Limit the use of educational jargon. Explain things in easy-to-understand language.
7. Use professional ethics and conduct at all times.
8. Keep all information discussed at the conference confidential.
9. Remain as calm as possible, and keep your cool if a parent becomes hostile. Ask the parent if he would like to speak to the principal, if appropriate. Otherwise report the incident to an administrator for future reference.
10. Relax.

# For Further Reading

## BOOKS ON PUBERTY FOR EARLY ADOLESCENTS

The following books have been written specifically for early adolescent children. The purpose of these books is to educate children about their changing bodies during puberty. An introduction to the book or a message to parents is included in each book. Previewing a book before passing it along to a child is strongly recommended.

Dobson, James. *Preparing for Adolescence*. New York: Bantam Books, 1978.

Suitable for 10- to 15-year-olds. Discusses physical change and development, but the emphasis is on social and emotional development from a Christian point of view. Includes biblical quotes that relate to various problem areas of preteen and adolescent life, behavior, and development. No illustrations.

Madaras, Lynda. *What's Happening to My Body? Book for Girls*. New York: Newmarket Press, 1988.
Madaras, Lynda. *What's Happening to My Body? Book for Boys*. New York: Newmarket Press, 1988.

Award-winning books written in conversational style. Written for 9- to 14-year-olds but most suitable for 11- to 14-year-olds. Deals with puberty and physical changes as well as sexuality. Illustrated. Question and answer section. Anecdotes. More comprehensive than other books.

## BOOKS ON PUBERTY FOR PARENTS AND CHILDREN TO READ TOGETHER

Chirinian, Alain. *Boys' Puberty: An Illustrated Manual for Parents and Sons*. New York: Tom Doherty Associates, 1990.
Hynes, Angela. *Puberty: An Illustrated Manual for Parents and Daughters*. New York: Tom Doherty Associates, 1990.

Books simply written and illustrated for both parent and daughter, or parent and son, to read. Deals with physical and sexual development. Discussion of common problems and myths young girls/boys have about physical or sexual development through a series of ministories at the end of each book. Most suitable for 9- to 12-year-olds.

Sullivan, Maria. *Peer Pressure*. New York: Tom Doherty Associates, 1991.

A book simply written and illustrated with anecdotes for both parent and child to read about peer pressure and how to deal with it.

## ADDITIONAL READING FOR PARENTS AND ADULTS

Bayard, Robert and Jean. *How to Deal with Your Acting Up Teenager*. New York: M. Evans and Co. Inc., 1983.
Clarke, Jean Illsby. *Help for Parents of Teenagers*. San Francisco: Harper and Row, 1986.

Dinkmeyer, Don, and Gary McKay. *Parenting Teenagers*. Circle Pines, Minnesota: American Guidance Service, 1990.

Ginott, Haim. *Between Parent and Teenager*. New York: Macmillan, 1971.

Gross, Leonard, ed. *The Parents Guide to Teenagers*. New York: Macmillan, 1981.

Kirshenbaum, Mira, and Charles Foster. *Parent/Teen Breakthrough*. New York: Penguin Books, 1991.

Powell, Douglas. *Teenagers: When to Worry and What to Do*. New York: Doubleday and Co., 1986.

Steinberg, Laurence, and Ann Levine. *You and Your Adolescent: A Parents Guide for Ages 10 to 20*. New York: Harper Perennial, 1990.

Vedral, Joyce. *My Teenager Is Driving Me Crazy*. New York: Ballantine Books, 1989.

Weinhaus, Evonne, and Karen Friedman. *Stop Struggling with Your Teen*. New York: Penguin Books, 1988.

Wells, Joel. *How to Survive with Your Teenager*. Chicago: Thomas More Press, 1982.

## LITERATURE (FICTION BOOKS) FOR EARLY ADOLESCENTS

These fictional books about early adolescent lives and problems are written for the early adolescent age group. They are available through public libraries, school libraries, and bookstores. Previewing these books before using them in the classroom or passing them along to children is strongly recommended.

Anderson, Margaret, *The Journey of the Shadow Bairns*
Baer, Edith, *Sometimes I Think I Hear My Name*
Blue, Rose, *Grandma Didn't Wave Back*
Blume, Judy, *Are You There God? It's Me Margaret; It's Not the End of the World; Tales of a Fourth Grade Nothing; Then Again, Maybe I Won't; Otherwise Known as Sheila the Great; Blubber; Deenie; Superfudge*

Brides, Sue, *Home Before Dark*
Buchan, Bryan, *Copper Sunrise*
Burch, Robert, *Queenie Peavy*
Byars, Betsy, *Animal, Vegetable and John D. Jones; The Cybil War; The Pinballs; Summer of the Swans*
Childress, Alice, *A Hero Ain't Nothing but a Sandwich*
Conford, Ellen, *Felicia the Critic; Seven Days to a Brand New Me; Anything for a Friend*
Corbett, Scott, *Here Lies the Body*
Danziger, Paula, *Can You Sue Your Parents for Malpractice?; The Cat Ate My Gymsuit; There's a Bat in Bunk Five; The Pistachio Prescription*
DeClements, Barthe, *Nothing's Fair in Fifth Grade*
Gilson, Jamie, *Do Bananas Chew Gum?*
Girion, Barbara, *A Handful of Stars*
Greene, Bette, *Phillip Hall Likes Me, I Reckon Maybe*
Greene, Constance, *The Ears of Louis; Getting Nowhere; The Unmaking of Rabbit*
Hahn, Mary Downing, *Daphne's Book*
Hautzig, Ester, *The Endless Steppe*
Hentoff, Nat, *This School Is Driving Me Crazy*
Hinton, S. E., *That Was Then, This Is Now*
Holland, Isabelle, *Now Is Not Too Late*
Holman, Felice, *Slake's Limbo*
Jones, Hettie, *You Light Up My Life*
Kerr, M. E., *Is That You, Miss Blue?*
Klein, Norma, *It's Not What You Expect; It's OK If You Don't Love Me; Taking Sides*
Konigsburg, E. L., *From the Mixed-up Files of Mrs. Basil Frankweiler*
Levy, Elizabeth, *The Case of the Counterfeit Racehorse*
Lowry, Lois, *Anastasia Krupnik*
Mann, Peggy, *There Are Two Kinds of Terrible*
Mathis, Sharon Bell, *Teacup Full of Roses*
Miles, Betty, *All It Takes Is Practice; The Trouble with Thirteen*
Montgomery, R. *Yellow Eyes*
Mowat, Farley, *Never Cry Wolf*

Myers, Dean Walter, *Won't Know Till I Get There*
Neufeld, John, *Lisa Bright and Dark*
Pascal, Francine, *The Hand Me Down Kid*
Patterson, Katharine, *Bridge to Terabithia*
Pfeiffer, Susan, *What Do You Do When Your Mouth Won't Open?*
Phipson, John, *Fly into Danger*
Platt, Ken, *Chloris and the Creeps*
Rockwell, Thomas, *How to Eat Fried Worms*
Roth, Arthur, *Two for Survival*
Smith, Doris Buchanan, *Dreams and Drummers*; *Kelly's Creek*; *Last Was Lloyd*; *A Taste of Blackberries*
Snyder, Anne, *My Name Is Davy: I'm an Alcoholic*
Stevens, Carla, *Trouble for Lucy*
Taylor, Theodore, *The Cay*
Voigt, Cynthia, *Homecoming*; *Dicey's Song*; *The Runner*; *Izzy Willy-Nilly*
Zindel, B. and P., *A Star for a Latecomer*
Zindel, Paul, *Confessions of a Teenage Baboon*; *My Darling, My Hamburger*; *The Pigman*; *Pardon Me, Your Stepping on My Eyeball*

## JOURNALS FOR MIDDLE-LEVEL EDUCATORS

The following is a list of national journals that are available to middle-level teachers and educators.

*Middle School Journal*, National Middle School Association, Columbus, OH
*Clearing House*, Heldref Publications, Washington, DC
*Instructor Middle Years*, Scholastic, New York, NY
*Educational Oasis*, Good Apple, Carthage, IL

There are also journals on middle-level education published by many state-level middle school associations and by some National Council of Teachers organizations. For example, The National Council of Teachers of English publishes *Voices from the*

*Middle,* and The National Council of Teachers of Mathematics publishes *Mathematics Teaching in the Middle School.*

Other journals that include some articles on middle-level education include:

*Educational Leadership,* Association for Supervision and Curriculum Development, Alexandria, VA

*Teaching/K–8,* Norwalk, CT

# Index